Theory Test Questions
for Motorcyclists

2003–2004

Theory Test Questions for Motorcyclists

2003–2004

All the questions and answers valid
for motorcycle tests taken after July 1, 2003

Published by BSM in association with
Virgin Publishing

First published in the UK in 2003 by
The British School of Motoring Ltd
1 Forest Road
Feltham
Middlesex
TW13 7RR

ISBN 0 7535 0880 X

Design, typesetting and reprographics by Thalamus Publishing

Printed in Italy

Contents

Foreword

Riding a motorcycle is a valuable life skill, which is why every year between 200,000 and 250,000 new learners take to the road. Unlike learning to drive a car – where undoubtedly everyone's aim is to gain their full licence – people can ride some scooters and motorcycles unaccompanied on a provisional motorcycle licence after having only completed a Compulsory Basic Training course, depending on their age. As the popularity of motorcycles increases due to reasons such as traffic congestion, the cost of motoring, and the unreliability of public transport, training and safety must be at the top of the list for anyone contemplating two wheels as a mode of transport.

There is no substitute for practical experience when learning to ride. The best way to gain this is by taking lessons with a good professional motorcycle instructor who uses the most up-to-date teaching techniques and modern radio-equipped motorcycles.

In many ways, the training and testing of motorcyclists is more heavily regulated than learning to drive. Already there are three stages to obtaining a full motorcycle licence:

stage 1
Compulsory Basic Training (CBT)

stage 2
The Motorcycle Theory Test including the more recently introduced Hazard Perception element.*

stage 3
The practical on-road test.**

Only stage 1 needs to be achieved if a full licence is not the objective, but there is nothing to prevent you studying and

* CBT and the Theory Test can be taken in any order and the theory test is not required if a practical test is not being taken. BSM would, however, advise everyone to take the Theory Test.

** The introduction of an extension to the current practical test or a further testing stage, including a hazard avoidance exercise and a compulsory slow riding exercise, is under discussion. At the time of going to press no firm conclusion had been reached.

passing the Theory Test. Doing so will improve your knowledge and skills, and therefore your safety and that of others. To get a full motorcycle licence, it is required that you pass the Motorcycle Theory Test before taking the Practical Test (whether or not you already have passed the car Theory Test and/or hold a full car licence). Preparation for your riding lessons is very important, and this is doubly true since the introduction of the Motorcycle Theory Test.

The BSM book Theory Test Questions for Motorcyclists contains the revised set of official Driving Standards Agency questions (valid for tests after July 1, 2003) and which may be included in the actual examination. This book is an ideal study aid, which allows you to test and revise your knowledge.

Theory Test Questions for Motorcyclists allows you to check your level of knowledge by presenting you with real examination questions. The questions are set out under topic headings. As you work through each section you will prove to yourself that you understand what you have learnt, and you can demonstrate this by answering the questions correctly. In doing so, you will gradually boost your confidence and thereby recognise when you are ready to take and pass your Motorcycle Theory Test.

Your instructor will help you to plan your studies and ensure that you fully understand why the knowledge you

acquire is essential to keep you safe on the road, as well as to take you past that all important hurdle of passing the Motorcycle Theory Test.

There are no short cuts to becoming a safe and competent motorcyclist, but that does not mean that you cannot enjoy yourself while learning. BSM has over 90 years of experience teaching people to drive, and has more recently transferred those skills to motorcycle training. To book motorcycle training or obtain advice, all you have to do is call us on 0870 902 1700.

Theory Test Questions for Motorcyclists is a vital aid to anyone learning to ride a motorcycle at any level. It will ensure that you make the most of your training and will prepare you for the theory and practical parts of your training, Theory and Practical Tests.

At the end of this book, there is some useful information covering CBT, routes to a full licence, clothing and much more. This section offers some very valuable guidance at the early stages of your motorcycling experience.

Motorcycling is one of the most enjoyable and exciting forms of transport or it can merely be a means to an end to get from A to B. Whatever your motivation or reasons for deciding to ride a motorcycle, this book will help you gain confidence and knowledge and help make you into a safer rider.

Introduction

Some riders view the Theory Test only as an irrelevant exam which you have to do on the way to getting a full licence. However, learning answers to questions without understanding the meaning will not improve your skills and is not the best way to pass your Motorcycle Theory Test. You need to think clearly about what answer the question is looking for and then make sure that you understand how that answer can assist your practical riding skills.

Until February 2001, full car-licence holders were exempt from taking the separate Motorcycle Theory test if they wanted to take a Motorcycle Practical Test. Although the sequence of traffic lights is no different when riding a motorcycle than if you were driving a car, there are other significant differences. This was the reason that, with effect from February 2001, anyone wanting a full motorcycle licence is required to take the Motorcycle Theory Test.

Remember when you actually sit the Theory Test you will have plenty of time to read the questions thoroughly. Make sure you understand what is being asked. Don't rush or panic; instead think carefully about each suggested answer.

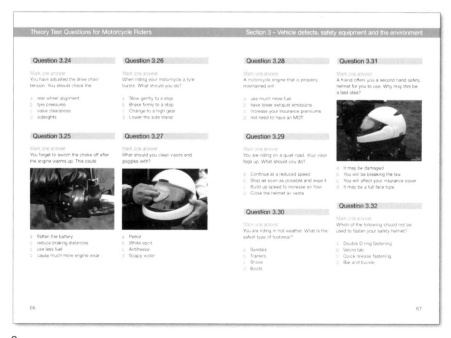

8

Invariably, if you have put the time and effort into studying, the correct answer or answers should be more than apparent. If you have queries or areas that you do not understand, you should ask your instructor.

This book contains all 790 of the official multiple-choice questions for motorcyclists that make up the current DSA question bank. In your Theory Test, you will be asked 35 of these questions. You need to provide the correct answers to at least 30 in order to pass the multiple-choice element of the Theory Test. At the Test Centre, you sit at a computer and the questions appear on the computer screen. You select your answers by simply touching the screen. This touch-screen system has been carefully designed to make it easy to use.

The second element of the Theory Test is Hazard Perception. In this part of the Test, you are shown video footage of real road situations and you are expected to quickly identify developing hazards. Whereas the multiple-choice section of the Test assesses your knowledge and understanding, the Hazard Perception section tests your awareness and skills. Therefore, you need to prepare for this part of the Test in a different way. BSM has several publications and computer-based training aids which have been specially designed to help with your preparation; for details of these, or for

more information about the Hazard Perception test, visit www.bsm.co.uk or call us on 08457 276276. Remember that you need to pass Hazard Perception at the same sitting as the multiple-choice section of the Test, otherwise you need to take the whole Test again.

The important point about the Theory Test is that it is not an irrelevant exam. All parts of the Test are interconnected with the practical elements of your rider training and all contribute to making you a better, safer rider. Proper study and understanding of the subjects covered by both parts of the Theory Test will also be a great help in securing a pass on the Practical Test.

Note: Questions marked NI Exempt are not part of the Motorcycle Theory Test in Northern Ireland

9

Theory Test Questions for Motorcyclists

2003–2004

Section 1   Alertness

Question 1.1

Mark two answers
You want to change lanes in busy, moving traffic. Why could looking over your shoulder help?

a Mirrors may not cover blind spots
b To avoid having to give a signal
c So traffic ahead will make room for you
d So your balance will not be affected
e Following motorists would be warned

Question 1.2

Mark one answer
You are about to turn right. What should you do just before you turn?

a Give the correct signal
b Take a 'lifesaver' glance over your shoulder
c Select the correct gear
d Get in position ready for the turn

Question 1.3

Mark one answer
What is the 'lifesaver' when riding a motorcycle?

a A certificate every motorcyclist must have
b A final, rearward glance before changing direction
c A part of the motorcycle tool kit
d A mirror fitted to check blind spots

Question 1.4

Mark one answer
You see road signs showing a sharp bend ahead. What should you do?

a Continue at the same speed
b Slow down as you go around the bend
c Slow down as you come out of the bend
d Slow down before the bend

Question 1.5

Mark one answer
You are riding at night and are dazzled by the headlights of an oncoming car. You should

a slow down or stop
b close your eyes
c flash your headlight
d turn your head away

Question 1.6

Mark one answer
When riding, your shoulders obstruct the view in your mirrors. To overcome this you should

a indicate earlier than normal
b fit smaller mirrors
c extend the mirror arms
d brake earlier than normal

12

Question 1.7

Mark one answer

On a motorcycle you should only use a mobile telephone when you

a have a pillion passenger to help
b have parked in a safe place
c have a motorcycle with automatic gears
d are travelling on a quiet road

Question 1.8

Mark one answer

You are riding along a motorway. You see an accident on the other side of the road. Your lane is clear. You should

a assist the emergency services
b stop, and cross the road to help
c concentrate on what is happening ahead
d place a warning triangle in the road

Question 1.9

Mark one answer

You are riding at night. You have your headlight on main beam. Another vehicle is overtaking you. When should you dip your headlight?

a When the other vehicle signals to overtake
b As soon as the other vehicle moves out to overtake
c As soon as the other vehicle passes you
d After the other vehicle pulls in front of you

Question 1.10

Mark one answer

To move off safely from a parked position you should

a signal if other drivers will need to slow down
b leave your motorcycle on its stand until the road is clear
c give an arm signal as well as using your indicators
d look over your shoulder for a final check

13

Question 1.11

In motorcycling, the term 'lifesaver' refers to

a a final rearward glance
b an approved safety helmet
c a reflective jacket
d the two-second rule

Question 1.12

Riding a motorcycle when you are cold could cause you to

a be more alert
b be more relaxed
c react more quickly
d lose concentration

Question 1.13

You are riding at night and are dazzled by the lights of an approaching vehicle.
What should you do?

a Switch off your headlight
b Switch to main beam
c Slow down and stop
d Flash your headlight

Question 1.14

You should always check the 'blind areas' before

a moving off
b slowing down
c changing gear
d giving a signal

Question 1.15

The 'blind area' should be checked before

a giving a signal
b applying the brakes
c changing direction
d giving an arm signal

Question 1.16

It is vital to check the 'blind area' before

a changing gear
b giving signals
c slowing down
d changing lanes

Question 1.17

Mark one answer

You are about to emerge from a junction. Your pillion passenger tells you it's clear. When should you rely on their judgement?

a   Never you should always look for yourself
b   When the roads are very busy
c   When the roads are very quiet
d   Only when they are a qualified rider

Question 1.18

Mark one answer

You are about to emerge from a junction. Your pillion passenger tells you it's safe to go. What should you do?

a   Go if you are sure they can see clearly
b   Check for yourself before pulling out
c   Take their advice and ride on
d   Ask them to check again before you go

Question 1.19

Mark one answer

What must you do before stopping normally?

a   Put both feet down
b   Select 1st gear
c   Use your mirrors
d   Move into neutral

Question 1.20

Mark one answer

You have been waiting for some time to make a right turn into a side road. What should you do just before you make the turn?

a   Move close to the kerb
b   Select a higher gear
c   Make a lifesaver check
d   Wave to the oncoming traffic

Question 1.21

Mark one answer

You are turning right onto a dual carriageway. What should you do before emerging?

a   Stop and then select a very low gear
b   Position in the left gutter of the side road
c   Check that the central reserve is wide enough
d   Check there is enough room for following vehicles

15

Question 1.22

Mark one answer
When riding a different motorcycle you should

a ask someone to ride with you for the first time
b ride as soon as possible as all controls and switches are the same
c leave your gloves behind so switches can be operated easier at first
d be sure you know where all controls and switches are

Question 1.23

Mark one answer
Why can it be helpful to have mirrors fitted on each side of your motorcycle?

a To judge the gap when filtering in traffic
b To give protection when riding in poor weather
c To make your motorcycle appear larger to other drivers
d To give you the best view of the road behind

Question 1.24

Mark one answer
Before you make a U-turn in the road, you should

a give an arm signal as well as using your indicators
b signal so that other drivers can slow down for you
c look over your shoulder for a final check
d select a higher gear than normal

Question 1.25

Mark three answers
As you approach this bridge you should

a move into the middle of the road to get a better view
b slow down
c get over the bridge as quickly as possible
d consider using your horn
e find another route
f beware of pedestrians

Question 1.26

Mark one answer
When following a large vehicle you should keep well back because

a   it allows you to corner more quickly
b   it helps the large vehicle to stop more easily
c   it allows the driver to see you in the mirrors
d   it helps you to keep out of the wind

Question 1.27

Mark one answer
In which of these situations should you avoid overtaking?

a   Just after a bend
b   In a one-way street
c   On a 30mph road
d   Approaching a dip in the road

Question 1.28

Mark one answer
This road marking warns

a   drivers to use the hard shoulder
b   overtaking drivers there is a bend to the left
c   overtaking drivers to move back to the left
d   drivers that it is safe to overtake

Question 1.29

Mark one answer
Your mobile phone rings while you are travelling. You should

a   stop immediately
b   answer it immediately
c   pull up in a suitable place
d   pull up at the nearest kerb

Question 1.30

Why are these yellow lines painted across the road?

a   To help you choose the correct lane
b   To help you keep the correct separation distance
c   To make you aware of your speed
d   To tell you the distance to the roundabout

Question 1.31

You are approaching traffic lights that have been on green for some time. You should

a   accelerate hard
b   maintain your speed
c   be ready to stop
d   brake hard

Question 1.32

Which of the following should you do before stopping?

a   Sound the horn
b   Use the mirrors
c   Select a higher gear
d   Flash your headlights

Answers and explanations

1.1   a, e

1.2   b

1.3   b

1.4   d

1.5   a

1.6   c Mirrors should be adjusted to give you the best view of the road behind. If your shoulders or elbows obstruct the view behind you should fit alternative mirrors with longer stems.

1.7   b

1.8   c

1.9   c

1.10   d

1.11   a

1.12   d

1.13   c

1.14   a Before moving off you should check over your right shoulder to make sure that no one is there who could not be seen in your mirrors.

1.15   c

1.16   d A motorcyclist or cyclist could be hidden in the blind area and not visible in your mirrors. A quick sideways glance before changing lanes ensures that it is safe.

1.17   a A pillion rider will not have the same line of vision as you and should never be relied on to judge a road condition.

1.18   b

1.19   c

1.20   c If you have been stationary for some time there is a chance that another vehicle will have positioned themselves in your blind spot.

1.21   c A narrow central reservation could mean part of your vehicle is obstructing the flow of trafic on the major road.

1.22   d

1.23   d

1.24   c You should always check your blind spot just before moving off or starting a manoeuvre.

1.25   b, d, f

1.26   c

1.27   d

1.28   c

1.29   c

1.30   c

1.31   c

1.32   b

Section 2

Attitudes to other road users

Question 2.1

Mark one answer

You are riding towards a zebra crossing. Pedestrians are waiting to cross. You should

a give way to the elderly and infirm only
b slow down and prepare to stop
c use your headlight to indicate they can cross
d wave at them to cross the road

Question 2.2

Mark one answer

You are riding a motorcycle and following a large vehicle at 40mph. You should position yourself

a close behind to make it easier to overtake the vehicle
b to the left of the road to make it easier to be seen
c close behind the vehicle to keep out of the wind
d well back so that you can see past the vehicle

Question 2.3

Mark one answer

You are riding on a country road. Two horses with riders are in the distance. You should

a continue at your normal speed
b change down the gears quickly
c slow down and be ready to stop
d flash your headlight to warn them

Question 2.4

Mark one answer

You are approaching a red light at a puffin crossing. Pedestrians are on the crossing. The red light will stay on until

a you start to edge forward on to the crossing
b the pedestrians have reached a safe position
c the pedestrians are clear of the front of your motorcycle
d a driver from the opposite direction reaches the crossing

Question 2.5

Mark one answer

You are riding a slow-moving scooter on a narrow, winding road. You should

a keep well out to stop vehicles overtaking dangerously

b wave following vehicles past you if you think they can overtake quickly

c pull in safely when you can, to let following vehicles overtake

d give a left signal when it is safe for vehicles to overtake you

Question 2.6

Mark two answers

When riding a motorcycle your normal road position should allow

a other vehicles to overtake on your left

b the driver ahead to see you in the mirrors

c you to prevent following vehicles from overtaking

d you to be seen by traffic that is emerging from junctions ahead

e you to ride within half a metre (1 foot 8 ins) of the kerb

Question 2.7

Mark one answer

At a pelican crossing the flashing amber light means you MUST

a stop and wait for the green light

b stop and wait for the red light

c give way to pedestrians waiting to cross

d give way to pedestrians already on the crossing

Question 2.8

Mark one answer

You should never wave people across at pedestrian crossings because

a there may be another vehicle coming

b they may not be looking

c it is safer for you to carry on

d they may not be ready to cross

Question 2.9

Mark one answer

At a puffin crossing what colour follows the green signal?

a Steady red

b Flashing amber

c Steady amber

d Flashing green

Question 2.10

Mark one answer
You could use the 'Two-Second Rule'

a   before restarting the engine after it has stalled
b   to keep a safe gap from the vehicle in front
c   before using the 'Mirror-Signal-Manoeuvre' routine
d   when emerging on wet roads

Question 2.11

Mark one answer
Following this vehicle too closely is unwise because

a   your brakes will overheat
b   your view ahead is increased
c   your engine will overheat
d   your view ahead is reduced

Question 2.12

Mark one answer
'Tailgating' means

a   using the rear door of a hatchback car
b   reversing into a parking space
c   following another vehicle too closely
d   driving with rear fog lights on

Question 2.13

Mark one answer
You are following a vehicle on a wet road. You should leave a time gap of at least

a   one second
b   two seconds
c   three seconds
d   four seconds

Question 2.14

Mark one answer
You are in a line of traffic. The driver behind you is following very closely. What action should you take?

a   Ignore the following driver and continue to drive within the speed limit
b   Slow down, gradually increasing the gap between you and the vehicle in front
c   Signal left and wave the following driver past
d   Move over to a position just left of the centre line of the road

Question 2.15

Mark one answer

A long, heavily-laden lorry is taking a long time to overtake you. What should you do?

a   Speed up
b   Slow down
c   Hold your speed
d   Change direction

Question 2.16

Mark three answers

Which of the following vehicles will use blue flashing beacons?

a   Motorway maintenance
b   Bomb disposal
c   Blood transfusion
d   Police patrol
e   Breakdown recovery

Question 2.17

Mark three answers

Which THREE of these emergency services might have blue flashing beacons?

a   Coastguard
b   Bomb disposal
c   Gritting lorries
d   Animal ambulances
e   Mountain rescue
f   Doctors' cars

Question 2.18

Mark one answer

When being followed by an ambulance showing a flashing blue beacon you should

a   pull over as soon as safely possible to let it pass
b   accelerate hard to get away from it
c   maintain your speed and course
d   brake harshly and immediately stop in the road

Question 2.19

Mark one answer

What type of emergency vehicle is fitted with a green flashing beacon?

a   Fire engine
b   Road gritter
c   Ambulance
d   Doctor's car

Question 2.20

Mark one answer

A flashing green beacon on a vehicle means

a   police on non-urgent duties
b   doctor on an emergency call
c   road safety patrol operating
d   gritting in progress

Question 2.21

Mark one answer
A vehicle has a flashing green beacon. What does this mean?

a   A doctor is answering an emergency call
b   The vehicle is slow-moving
c   It is a motorway police patrol vehicle
d   A vehicle is carrying hazardous chemicals

Question 2.22

Mark one answer
Diamond-shaped signs give instructions to

a   tram drivers
b   bus drivers
c   lorry drivers
d   taxi drivers

Question 2.23

Mark one answer
On a road where trams operate, which of these vehicles will be most at risk from the tram rails?

a   Cars
b   Cycles
c   Buses
d   Lorries

Question 2.24

Mark one answer
What should you use your horn for?

a   To alert others to your presence
b   To allow you right of way
c   To greet other road users
d   To signal your annoyance

Question 2.25

Mark one answer
You are in a one-way street and want to turn right. You should position yourself

a   in the right-hand lane
b   in the left-hand lane
c   in either lane, depending on the traffic
d   just left of the centre line

Question 2.26

You wish to turn right ahead. Why should you take up the correct position in good time?

a To allow other drivers to pull out in front of you
b To give a better view into the road that you're joining
c To help other road users know what you intend to do
d To allow drivers to pass you on the right

Question 2.27

At which type of crossing are cyclists allowed to ride across with pedestrians?

a Toucan
b Puffin
c Pelican
d Zebra

Question 2.28

A bus is stopped at a bus stop ahead of you. Its right-hand indicator is flashing. You should

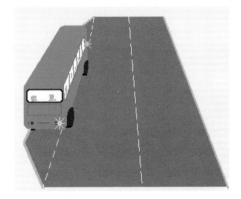

a flash your headlights and slow down
b slow down and give way if it is safe to do so
c sound your horn and keep going
d slow down and then sound your horn

Question 2.29

You are travelling at the legal speed limit. A vehicle comes up quickly behind, flashing its headlights. You should

a accelerate to make a gap behind you
b touch the brakes sharply to show your brake lights
c maintain your speed to prevent the vehicle from overtaking
d allow the vehicle to overtake

Question 2.30

Mark one answer
You should ONLY flash your headlights to other road users

a   to show that you are giving way
b   to show that you are about to turn
c   to tell them that you have right of way
d   to let them know that you are there

Question 2.31

Mark one answer
You are approaching unmarked crossroads. How should you deal with this type of junction?

a   Accelerate and keep to the middle
b   Slow down and keep to the right
c   Accelerate looking to the left
d   Slow down and look both ways

Question 2.32

Mark one answer
You are approaching a pelican crossing. The amber light is flashing. You must

a   give way to pedestrians who are crossing
b   encourage pedestrians to cross
c   not move until the green light appears
d   stop even if the crossing is clear

Answers and explanations

2.1   b

2.2   d If you can see past the vehicle you can decide whether it is safe to overtake.

2.3   c Take extra care where there are horses around as they can easily be alarmed.

2.4   b

2.5   c

2.6   b, d

2.7   d

2.8   a

2.9   c

2.10   b A two-second time gap from the vehicle in front provides a safe gap in good conditions.

2.11   d If you hang back you will have a much better view of the road ahead.

2.12   c

2.13   d In good conditions you should allow two seconds but on a wet road you double this to four.

2.14   b By increasing the gap between you and the vehicle in front, you give yourself and the driver behind more room to stop should you need it.

2.15   b By slowing down, you allow the lorry to get past, which is the only safe option.

2.16   b, ,c, d

2.17   a, b, e

2.18   a

2.19   d Doctors on emergency call may display a flashing green beacon. Slow-moving vehicles have amber flashing beacons. Police, fire and ambulance service vehicles have blue flashing beacons.

2.20   b

2.21   a

2.22   a

2.23   b

2.24   a

2.25   a

2.26   c The position of your motorcycle helps signal your intentions to other road users.

2.27   a

2.28   b

2.29   d This is your only safe option.

2.30   d

2.31   d At an unmarked crossroads no one has the priority and caution is required.

2.32   a You must give way to pedestrians already on the crossing but may drive on if the crossing is clear.

heory Test Questions
or Motorcyclists

2003–2004

Section 3   Motorcycle defects,
safety equipment
and the environment

Question 3.1

Mark one answer
A loose drive chain on a motorcycle could cause

a   the front wheel to wobble
b   the ignition to cut out
c   the brakes to fail
d   the rear wheel to lock

Question 3.2

Mark three answers
A wrongly adjusted drive chain can

a   cause an accident
b   make wheels wobble
c   create a noisy rattle
d   affect gear changing
e   cause a suspension fault

Question 3.3

Mark one answer
What is the most important reason why you should keep your motorcycle regularly maintained?

a   To accelerate faster than other traffic
b   So the motorcycle can carry panniers
c   To keep the machine roadworthy
d   So the motorcycle can carry a passenger

Question 3.4

Mark one answer
Your motorcycle has tubed tyres fitted as standard. When replacing a tyre you should

a   replace the tube if it is 6 months old
b   replace the tube if it has covered 6,000 miles
c   replace the tube only if replacing the rear tyre
d   replace the tube with each change of tyre

Question 3.5

Mark one answer
How should you ride a motorcycle when NEW tyres have just been fitted?

a   Carefully, until the shiny surface is worn off
b   By braking hard especially into bends
c   Through normal riding with higher air pressures
d   By riding at faster than normal speeds

Question 3.6

Mark one answer
Which of the following would NOT make you more visible in daylight?

a   A black helmet
b   A white helmet
c   Switching on your dipped headlamp
d   Wearing a fluorescent jacket

Question 3.7

Mark one answer
When riding and wearing brightly coloured clothing you will

a   dazzle other motorists on the road
b   be seen more easily by other motorists
c   create a hazard by distracting other drivers
d   be able to ride on unlit roads at night with sidelights

Question 3.8

Mark one answer
You are riding a motorcycle in very hot weather. You should

a   ride with your visor fully open
b   continue to wear protective clothing
c   wear trainers instead of boots
d   slacken your helmet strap

Question 3.9

Mark one answer
Why should you wear fluorescent clothing when riding in daylight?

a   It reduces wind resistance
b   It prevents injury if you come off the machine
c   It helps other road users to see you
d   It keeps you cool in hot weather

Question 3.10

Mark one answer
Why should riders wear reflective clothing?

a   To protect them from the cold
b   To protect them from direct sunlight
c   To be seen better in daylight
d   To be seen better at night

Question 3.11

Mark one answer
Which of the following fairings would give you the best weather protection?

a   Handlebar
b   Sports
c   Touring
d   Windscreen

Question 3.12

Mark one answer

It would be illegal to ride WITH a helmet on when

a the helmet is not fastened correctly
b the helmet is more than four years old
c you have borrowed someone else's helmet
d the helmet does not have chin protection

Question 3.13

Mark one answer

Your visor becomes badly scratched. You should

a polish it with a fine abrasive
b replace it
c wash it in soapy water
d clean it with petrol

Question 3.14

Mark one answer

The legal minimum depth of tread for motorcycle tyres is

a 1 mm
b 1.6 mm
c 2.5 mm
d 4 mm

Question 3.15

Mark one answer

When MUST you use a dipped headlight during the day?

a On country roads
b In poor visibility
c Along narrow streets
d When parking

Question 3.16

Mark three answers

Which of the following makes it easier for motorcyclists to be seen?

a Using a dipped headlight
b Wearing a fluorescent jacket
c Wearing a white helmet
d Wearing a grey helmet
e Wearing black leathers
f Using a tinted visor

Question 3.17

Mark one answer

Tyre pressures should be increased on your motorcycle when

a riding on a wet road
b carrying a pillion passenger
c travelling on an uneven surface
d riding on twisty roads

34

Question 3.18

Mark one answer
Your oil light comes on as you are riding. You should

a go to a dealer for an oil change
b go to the nearest garage for their advice
c ride slowly for a few miles to see if the light goes out
d stop as quickly as possible and try to find the cause

Question 3.19

Mark three answers
When may you have to increase the tyre pressures on your motorcycle?

a When carrying a pillion passenger
b After a long journey
c When carrying heavy loads
d When riding at high speeds
e When riding in hot weather

Question 3.20

Mark two answers
Which TWO of these items on a motorcycle MUST be kept clean?

a Number plate
b Wheels
c Engine
d Fairing
e Headlights

Question 3.21

Mark two answers
Motorcycle tyres MUST

a have the same tread pattern
b be correctly inflated
c be the same size, front and rear
d both be the same make
e have sufficient tread depth

Question 3.22

Mark one answer
You should use the engine cut-out switch on your motorcycle to

a save wear and tear on the battery
b stop the engine on short stops
c stop the engine in an emergency
d save wear and tear on the ignition

Question 3.23

Mark one answer
Riding your motorcycle with a slack or worn drive chain may cause

a an engine misfire
b early tyre wear
c increased emissions
d a locked wheel

Question 3.24

Mark one answer
You have adjusted the drive chain tension. You should check the

a   rear wheel alignment
b   tyre pressures
c   valve clearances
d   sidelights

Question 3.25

Mark one answer
You forget to switch the choke off after the engine warms up. This could

a   flatten the battery
b   reduce braking distances
c   use less fuel
d   cause much more engine wear

Question 3.26

Mark one answer
When riding your motorcycle a tyre bursts. What should you do?

a   Slow gently to a stop
b   Brake firmly to a stop
c   Change to a high gear
d   Lower the side stand

Question 3.27

Mark one answer
What should you clean visors and goggles with?

a   Petrol
b   White spirit
c   Antifreeze
d   Soapy water

36

Question 3.28

Mark one answer

A motorcycle engine that is properly maintained will

a use much more fuel
b have lower exhaust emissions
c increase your insurance premiums
d not need to have an MOT

Question 3.29

Mark one answer

You are riding on a quiet road. Your visor fogs up. What should you do?

a Continue at a reduced speed
b Stop as soon as possible and wipe it
c Build up speed to increase air flow
d Close the helmet air vents

Question 3.30

Mark one answer

You are riding in hot weather. What is the safest type of footwear?

a Sandals
b Trainers
c Shoes
d Boots

Question 3.31

Mark one answer

A friend offers you a second-hand safety helmet for you to use. Why may this be a bad idea?

a It may be damaged
b You will be breaking the law
c You will affect your insurance cover
d It may be a full face type

Question 3.32

Mark one answer

Which of the following should not be used to fasten your safety helmet?

a Double D ring fastening
b Velcro tab
c Quick release fastening
d Bar and buckle

Question 3.33

Mark one answer
After warming up the engine you leave the choke ON. What will this do?

a Discharge the battery
b Use more fuel
c Improve handling
d Use less fuel

Question 3.34

Mark two answers
You want to ride your motorcycle in the dark. What could you wear to be seen more easily ?

a A black leather jacket
b Reflective clothing
c A white helmet
d A red helmet

Question 3.35

Mark four answers
You are riding a motorcycle of more than 50cc. Which FOUR would make a tyre illegal?

a Tread less than 1.6 mm deep
b Tread less than 1 mm deep
c A large bulge in the wall
d A recut tread
e Exposed ply or cord
f A stone wedged in the tread

Question 3.36

Mark two answers
You should maintain cable operated brakes

a by regular adjustment when necessary
b at normal service times only
c yearly, before taking the motorcycle for its MOT
d by oiling cables and pivots regularly

Question 3.37

Mark two answers
A properly serviced motorcycle will give

a lower insurance premiums
b you a refund on your road tax
c better fuel economy
d cleaner exhaust emissions

Question 3.38

Mark one answer

Your motorcycle has a catalytic converter. Its purpose is to reduce

a exhaust noise
b fuel consumption
c exhaust emissions
d engine noise

Question 3.39

Mark one answer

Refitting which of the following will disturb your wheel alignment?

a front wheel
b front brakes
c rear brakes
d rear wheel

Question 3.40

Mark one answer

After refitting your rear wheel what should you check?

a Your steering damper
b Your side stand
c Your wheel alignment
d Your suspension preload

Question 3.41

Mark one answer

You are checking your direction indicators. How often per second must they flash?

a Between 1 and 2 times
b Between 3 and 4 times
c Between 5 and 6 times
d Between 7 and 8 times

Question 3.42

Mark one answer

After adjusting the final drive chain what should you check?

a The rear wheel alignment
b The suspension adjustment
c The rear shock absorber
d The front suspension forks

Question 3.43

Mark one answer

Your steering feels wobbly. Which of these is a likely cause?

a Tyre pressure is too high
b Incorrectly adjusted brakes
c Worn steering head bearings
d A broken clutch cable

Question 3.44

Mark one answer
You see oil on your front forks. Should you be concerned about this?

a No, unless the amount of oil increases
b No, lubrication here is perfectly normal
c Yes, it is illegal to ride with an oil leak
d Yes, oil could drip onto your tyre

Question 3.45

Mark one answer
You have a faulty oil seal on a shock absorber. Why is this a serious problem?

a It will cause excessive chain wear
b Dripping oil could reduce the grip of your tyre
c Your motorcycle will be harder to ride uphill
d Your motorcycle will not accelerate so quickly

Question 3.46

Mark one answer
Oil is leaking from your forks. Why should you NOT ride a motorcycle in this condition?

a Your brakes could be affected by dripping oil
b Your steering is likely to seize up
c The forks will quickly begin to rust
d The motorcycle will become too noisy

Question 3.47

Mark one answer
You have adjusted your drive chain. If this is not done properly, what problem could it cause?

a Inaccurate speedometer reading
b Loss of braking power
c Incorrect rear wheel alignment
d Excessive fuel consumption

Question 3.48

Mark one answer
You have adjusted your drive chain. Why is it also important to check rear wheel alignment?

a Your tyre may be more likely to puncture
b Fuel consumption could be greatly increased
c You may not be able to reach top speed
d Your motorcycle could be unstable on bends

Question 3.49

Mark one answer
There is a cut in the sidewall of one of your tyres. What should you do about this?

a Replace the tyre before riding the motorcycle
b Check regularly to see if it gets any worse
c Repair the puncture before riding the motorcycle
d Reduce pressure in the tyre before you ride

Question 3.50

Mark one answer
You need to put air into your tyres. How would you find out the correct pressure to use?

a It will be shown on the tyre wall
b It will be stamped on the wheel
c By checking the vehicle owner's manual
d By checking the registration document

Question 3.51

Mark one answer
You can prevent a cable operated clutch from becoming stiff by keeping the cable

a tight
b dry
c slack
d oiled

Question 3.52

Mark one answer
When adusting your chain it is important for the wheels to be aligned accurately. Incorrect wheel alignment can cause

a a serious loss of power
b reduced braking performance
c increased tyre wear
d reduced ground clearance

41

Question 3.53

Mark one answer
What problem can incorrectly aligned wheels cause?

a   Faulty headlight adjustment
b   Reduced braking performance
c   Better ground clearance
d   Instability when cornering

Question 3.54

Mark one answer
What is most likely to be affected by incorrect wheel alignment?

a   Braking performance
b   Stability
c   Acceleration
d   Suspension preload

Question 3.55

Mark one answer
Why should you wear specialist motorcycle clothing when riding?

a   Because the law requires you to do so
b   Because it looks better than ordinary clothing
c   Because it gives best protection from the weather
d   Because it will reduce your insurance

Question 3.56

Mark one answer
When leaving your motorcycle parked, you should always

a   remove the battery lead
b   pull it onto the kerb
c   use the steering lock
d   leave the parking light on

Question 3.57

Mark one answer
You are parking your motorcycle. Chaining it to an immovable object will

a   be against the law
b   give extra security
c   be likely to cause damage
d   leave the motorcycle unstable

Question 3.58

Mark one answer
You are parking your motorcycle and sidecar on a hill. What is the best way to stop it rolling away?

a   Leave it in neutral
b   Put the rear wheel on the pavement
c   Leave it in a low gear
d   Park very close to another vehicle

Question 3.59

Mark one answer
An engine cut-out switch should be used to

a   reduce speed in an emergency
b   prevent the motorcycle being stolen
c   stop the engine normally
d   stop the engine in an emergency

Question 3.60

Mark one answer
You enter a road where there are road humps. What should you do?

a   Maintain a reduced speed throughout
b   Accelerate quickly between each one
c   Always keep to the maximum legal speed
d   Ride slowly at school times only

Question 3.61

Mark one answer
When should you especially check the engine oil level?

a   Before a long journey
b   When the engine is hot
c   Early in the morning
d   Every 6000 miles

Question 3.62

Mark one answer
You service your own motorcycle. How should you get rid of the old engine oil?

a   Take it to a local authority site
b   Pour it down a drain
c   Tip it into a hole in the ground
d   Put it into your dustbin

Question 3.63

Mark one answer
You are leaving your motorcycle parked on a road. When may you leave the engine running?

a   If you will be parked for less than five minutes
b   If the battery is flat
c   When in a 20mph zone
d   Not on any occasion

Question 3.64

Mark one answer
What safeguard could you take against fire risk to your motorcycle?

a   Keep water levels above maximum
b   Check out any strong smell of petrol
c   Avoid riding with a full tank of petrol
d   Use unleaded petrol

Question 3.65

Mark one answer
Which of these, if allowed to get low, could cause an accident?

a   Antifreeze level
b   Brake fluid level
c   Battery water level
d   Radiator coolant level

Question 3.66

Mark two answers
Which TWO are badly affected if the tyres are under-inflated?

a   Braking
b   Steering
c   Changing gear
d   Parking

Question 3.67

Mark three answers
Motor vehicles can harm the environment. This has resulted in

a   air pollution
b   damage to buildings
c   reduced health risks
d   improved public transport
e   less use of electrical vehicles
f   using up natural resources

Question 3.68

Mark three answers
Excessive or uneven tyre wear can be caused by faults in which THREE?

a   The gearbox
b   The braking system
c   The accelerator
d   The exhaust system
e   Wheel alignment
f   The suspension

Question 3.69

Mark one answer
You must NOT sound your horn

a between 10 pm and 6 am in a built-up area
b at any time in a built-up area
c between 11.30 pm and 7 am in a built-up area
d between 11.30 pm and 6 am on any road

Question 3.70

Mark three answers
The pictured vehicle is 'environmentally friendly' because it

a reduces noise pollution
b uses diesel fuel
c uses electricity
d uses unleaded fuel
e reduces parking spaces
f reduces town traffic

Question 3.71

Mark one answer
Supertrams or Light Rapid Transit (LRT) systems are environmentally friendly because

a they use diesel power
b they use quieter roads
c they use electric power
d they do not operate during rush hour

Question 3.72

Mark one answer
'Red routes' in major cities have been introduced to

a raise the speed limits
b help the traffic flow
c provide better parking
d allow lorries to load more freely

Question 3.73

Mark one answer
In some narrow, residential streets you will find a speed limit of

a 20mph
b 25mph
c 35mph
d 40mph

Question 3.74

Road humps, chicanes, and narrowings are

a   always at major road works
b   used to increase traffic speed
c   at toll-bridge approaches only
d   traffic calming measures

Question 3.75

The purpose of a catalytic converter is to reduce

a   fuel consumption
b   the risk of fire
c   toxic exhaust gases
d   engine wear

Question 3.76

Catalytic converters are fitted to make the

a   engine produce more power
b   exhaust system easier to replace
c   engine run quietly
d   exhaust fumes cleaner

Question 3.77

It is essential that tyre pressures are checked regularly. When should this be done?

a   After any lengthy journey
b   After travelling at high speed
c   When tyres are hot
d   When tyres are cold

Question 3.78

When should you NOT use your horn in a built-up area?

a   Between 8 pm and 8 am
b   Between 9 pm and dawn
c   Between dusk and 8 am
d   Between 11.30 pm and 7 am

Question 3.79

You will use more fuel if your tyres are

a   under-inflated
b   of different makes
c   over-inflated
d   new and hardly used

Question 3.80

Mark two answers
How should you dispose of a used battery?

a Take it to a local authority site
b Put it in the dustbin
c Break it up into pieces
d Leave it on waste land
e Take it to a garage
f Burn it on a fire

Question 3.81

Mark one answer
What is most likely to cause high fuel consumption?

a Poor steering control
b Accelerating around bends
c Staying in high gears
d Harsh braking and accelerating

Question 3.82

Mark one answer
The fluid level in your battery is low. What should you top it up with?

a Battery acid
b Distilled water
c Engine oil
d Engine coolant

Question 3.83

Mark one answer
You need top up your battery. What level should you fill to?

a The top of the battery
b Half-way up the battery
c Just below the cell plates
d Just above the cell plates

Question 3.84

Mark one answer
You have too much oil in your engine. What could this cause?

a Low oil pressure
b Engine overheating
c Chain wear
d Oil leaks

Question 3.85

Mark one answer
You are parking on a two-way road at night. The speed limit is 40mph. You should park on the

a left with parking lights on
b left with no lights on
c right with parking lights on
d right with dipped headlights on

Question 3.86

Mark one answer

You are parked on the road at night.
Where must you use parking lights?

a   Where there are continuous white
    lines in the middle of the road
b   Where the speed limit exceeds
    30mph
c   Where you are facing oncoming traffic
d   Where you are near a bus stop

3.1   d Drive chains require frequent
      adjustment and lubrication. If
      the chain is loose it can jump off
      the sprocket and lock the rear
      wheel.
3.2   a, c, d
3.3   c
3.4   d A punctured tyre should be
      properly repaired or replaced
      and if you have tubed tyres this
      means replacing the inner tyre
      as well.
3.5   a New tyres have a shiny surface
      which can reduce the grip. You
      need to ride carefully until the
      shiny surface is worn off. This
      could take up to 100 miles.
3.6   a
3.7   b
3.8   b Protective clothing offers some
      kind of protection against injury
      in the event of an accident.
3.9   c
3.10 d
3.11 c
3.12 a
3.13 b A badly scratched visor can
      distort your vision, causing
      dazzle from oncoming
      headlights at night and glare
      from a low winter sun.
3.14 a
3.15 b
3.16 a, b, c
3.17 b Inflate the tyres according to the
      maker's instruction.
3.18 d

3.19	a, c, d	3.45	b
3.20	a, e	3.46	a
3.21	b, e	3.47	c
3.22	c	3.48	d
3.23	d	3.49	a
3.24	a	3.50	c

3.25   d As soon as the engine warms up remember to push in the manual choke, otherwise the engine could be damaged and petrol will be wasted.

3.26   a With emergencies of this nature avoid sudden braking or changes of direction.

3.27   d Most other cleaning agents may have a solvent content, which will damage the visor.

3.51	d
3.52	c
3.53	d
3.54	b
3.55	c
3.56	c
3.57	b
3.58	c

3.28	b
3.29	b

3.30   d Whatever the weather conditions, full safety clothing should always be worn.

3.59   d This switch only isolates the engine. Lights, if in use, will remain on.

3.60   a Road humps are there to slow the traffic in residential areas.

3.31   a

3.32   b Velcro is only designed to tidy up more secure fastenings and would not be safe in an accident.

		3.61	a
		3.62	a
		3.63	d
3.33	b	3.64	b
3.34	b, c	3.65	b
3.35	b, c, d, e	3.66	a, b
3.36	a, d	3.67	a, b, f
3.37	c, d	3.68	b, e, f
3.38	c	3.69	c
3.39	d	3.70	a, c, f
3.40	c	3.71	c
3.41	a	3.72	b
3.42	a	3.73	a
3.43	c	3.74	d
3.44	d	3.75	c
		3.76	d
		3.77	d
		3.78	d
		3.79	a

49

3.80 a, e

3.81 d Harsh braking is one of the major causes of high fuel consumption.

3.82 b

3.83 d

3.84 d

3.85 a

3.86 b

Theory Test Questions for Motorcyclists

2003–2004

Section 4   Safety margins

Question 4.1

Mark one answer
Your overall stopping distance will be longer when riding

a at night
b in the fog
c with a passenger
d up a hill

Question 4.2

Mark one answer
Only a fool breaks the Two-Second Rule refers to

a the time recommended when using the choke
b the separation distance when riding in good conditions
c restarting a stalled engine in busy traffic
d the time you should keep your foot down at a junction

Question 4.3

Mark one answer
On a wet road what is the safest way to stop?

a Change gear without braking
b Use the back brake only
c Use the front brake only
d Use both brakes

Question 4.4

Mark one answer
You are riding in heavy rain when your rear wheel skids as you accelerate. To get control again you must

a change down to a lower gear
b ease off the throttle
c brake to reduce speed
d put your feet down

Question 4.5

Mark one answer
It is snowing. Before starting your journey you should

a think if you need to ride at all
b try to avoid taking a passenger
c plan a route avoiding towns
d take a hot drink before setting out

Question 4.6

Mark one answer
Why should you ride with a dipped headlight on in the daytime?

a It helps other road users to see you
b It means that you can ride faster
c Other vehicles will get out of the way
d So that it is already on when it gets dark

Question 4.7

Mark one answer
Motorcyclists are only allowed to use high-intensity rear fog lights when

a a pillion passenger is being carried
b they ride a large touring machine
c visibility is 100 metres (328 feet) or less
d they are riding on the road for the first time

Question 4.8

Mark two answers
When riding at night you should

a ride with your headlight on dipped beam
b wear reflective clothing
c wear a tinted visor
d ride in the centre of the road
e give arm signals

Question 4.9

Mark three answers
You MUST use your headlight

a when riding in a group
b at night when street lighting is poor
c when carrying a passenger
d on motorways during darkness
e at times of poor visibility
f when parked on an unlit road

Question 4.10

Mark one answer
You are riding in town at night. The roads are wet after rain. The reflections from wet surfaces will

a affect your stopping distance
b affect your road holding
c make it easy to see unlit objects
d make it hard to see unlit objects

Question 4.11

Mark two answers
You are riding through a flood. Which TWO should you do?

a Keep in a high gear and stand up on the footrests
b Keep the engine running fast to keep water out of the exhaust
c Ride slowly and test your brakes when you are out of the water
d Turn your headlight off to avoid any electrical damage

Question 4.12

Mark one answer
You have just ridden through a flood. When clear of the water you should test your

a starter motor
b headlight
c steering
d brakes

Question 4.13

Mark one answer

When going through flood water you should ride

a quickly in a high gear
b slowly in a high gear
c quickly in a low gear
d slowly in a low gear

Question 4.14

Mark one answer

When riding at night you should NOT

a switch on full beam headlights
b overtake slower vehicles in front
c use dipped beam headlights
d use tinted glasses, lenses or visors

Question 4.15

Mark one answer

At a mini roundabout it is important that a motorcyclist should avoid

a turning right
b using signals
c taking lifesavers
d the painted area

Question 4.16

Mark two answers

Which of the following should you do when riding in fog?

a Keep close to the vehicle in front
b Use your dipped headlight
c Ride close to the centre of the road
d Keep your visor or goggles clear
e Keep the vehicle in front in view

Question 4.17

Mark two answers

You are riding on a motorway in a crosswind. You should take extra care when

a approaching service areas
b overtaking a large vehicle
c riding in slow-moving traffic
d approaching an exit
e riding in exposed places

54

Question 4.18

You are riding in heavy rain. Why should you try to avoid this marked area?

a   It is illegal to ride over bus stops
b   The painted lines may be slippery
c   Cyclists may be using the bus stop
d   Only emergency vehicles may drive over bus stops

Question 4.19

Why should you try to avoid riding over this marked area?

a   It is illegal to ride over bus stops
b   It will alter your machine's centre of gravity
c   Pedestrians may be waiting at the bus stop
d   A bus may have left oil patches

Question 4.20

When riding at night you should

a   wear reflective clothing
b   wear a tinted visor
c   ride in the middle of the road
d   always give arm signals

Question 4.21

When riding in extremely cold conditions what can you do to keep warm?

a   Stay close to the vehicles in front
b   Wear suitable clothing
c   Lie flat on the tank
d   Put one hand on the exhaust pipe

Question 4.22

You are riding at night. To be seen more easily you should

a   ride with your headlight on dipped beam
b   wear reflective clothing
c   keep the motorcycle clean
d   stay well out to the right
e   wear waterproof clothing

Question 4.23

Mark one answer
Your overall stopping distance will be much longer when riding

a   in the rain
b   in fog
c   at night
d   in strong winds

Question 4.24

Mark four answers
The road surface is very important to motorcyclists. Which FOUR of these are more likely to reduce the stability of your motorcycle?

a   Potholes
b   Drain covers
c   Concrete
d   Oil patches
e   Tarmac
f   Loose gravel

Question 4.25

Mark two answers
You are riding in very hot weather. What are TWO effects that melting tar has on the control of your motorcycle?

a   It can make the surface slippery
b   It can reduce tyre grip
c   It can reduce stopping distances
d   It can improve braking efficiency

Question 4.26

Mark one answer
You are on a good, dry road surface. Your motorcycle has good brakes and tyres.What is the BRAKING distance at 50mph?

a   38 metres (125 feet)
b   14 metres (46 feet)
c   24 metres (79 feet)
d   55 metres (180 feet)

Question 4.27

Mark one answer
You are riding past queuing traffic. Why should you be more cautious when approaching this road marking?

a   Lorries will be unloading here
b   Schoolchildren will be crossing here
c   Pedestrians will be standing in the road
d   Traffic could be emerging and may not see you

Question 4.28

Mark one answer
What can cause your tyres to skid and lose their grip on the road surface?

a   Giving hand signals
b   Riding one-handed
c   Looking over your shoulder
d   Heavy braking

Question 4.29

Mark one answer
It has rained after a long dry spell. You should be very careful because the road surface will be unusually

a   loose
b   dry
c   sticky
d   slippery

Question 4.30

Mark one answer
You are riding at speed through surface water. A thin film of water has built up between your tyres and road surface. To keep control what should you do?

a   Turn the steering quickly
b   Use the rear brake gently
c   Use both brakes gently
d   Ease off the throttle

Question 4.31

Mark one answer
When riding in heavy rain a film of water can build up between your tyres and the road surface. This may result in loss of control. What can you do to avoid this happening?

a   Keep your speed down
b   Increase your tyre pressures
c   Decrease your tyre pressures
d   Keep trying your brakes

Question 4.32

Mark one answer
When riding in heavy rain a film of water can build up between your tyres and the road. This is known as aquaplaning. What should you do to keep control?

a   Use your rear brakes gently
b   Steer to the crown of the road
c   Ease off the throttle smoothly
d   Change up into a higher gear

Question 4.33

Mark one answer

You are on a good, dry road surface and your motorcycle has good brakes and tyres. What is the typical overall stopping distance at 40mph?

a 23 metres (75 feet)
b 36 metres (120 feet)
c 53 metres (175 feet)
d 96 metres (315 feet)

Question 4.34

Mark one answer

After riding through deep water you notice your scooter brakes do not work properly. What would be the best way to dry them out?

a Ride slowly, braking lightly
b Ride quickly, braking harshly
c Stop and dry them with a cloth
d Stop and wait for a few minutes

Question 4.35

Mark two answers

You have to ride in foggy weather. You should

a stay close to the centre of the road
b switch only your sidelights on
c switch on your dipped headlights
d be aware of others not using their headlights
e always ride in the gutter to see the kerb

Question 4.36

Mark one answer

Braking distances on ice can be

a twice the normal distance
b five times the normal distance
c seven times the normal distance
d ten times the normal distance

Question 4.37

Mark one answer

Freezing conditions will affect the distance it takes you to come to a stop. You should expect stopping distances to increase by up to

a two times
b three times
c five times
d ten times

Question 4.38

Mark two answers

In very hot weather the road surface can get soft. Which TWO of the following will be affected most?

a The suspension
b The grip of the tyres
c The braking
d The exhaust

Question 4.39

Mark one answer

Where are you most likely to be affected by a sidewind?

a On a narrow country lane
b On an open stretch of road
c On a busy stretch of road
d On a long, straight road

Question 4.40

Mark one answer

In windy conditions you need to take extra care when

a using the brakes
b making a hill start
c turning into a narrow road
d passing pedal cyclists

Question 4.41

Mark one answer

What is the shortest stopping distance at 70mph?

a 53 metres (175 feet)
b 60 metres (197 feet)
c 73 metres (240 feet)
d 96 metres (315 feet)

Question 4.42

Mark one answer

What is the shortest overall stopping distance on a dry road from 60mph?

a 53 metres (175 feet)
b 58 metres (190 feet)
c 73 metres (240 feet)
d 96 metres (315 feet)

Question 4.43

Mark one answer

Your indicators may be difficult to see in bright sunlight. What should you do?

a Put your indicator on earlier
b Give an arm signal as well as using your indicator
c Touch the brake several times to show the stop lights
d Turn as quickly as you can

Question 4.44

Mark one answer
When approaching a right-hand bend
you should keep well to the left.
Why is this?

a To improve your view of the road
b To overcome the effect of the road's
   slope
c To let faster traffic from behind
   overtake
d To be positioned safely if you skid

Question 4.45

Mark two answers
In very hot weather the road surface can
get soft. Which TWO of the following will
be affected most?

a The suspension
b The steering
c The braking
d The exhaust

Question 4.46

Mark three answers
You should not overtake when

a intending to turn left shortly afterwards
b in a one-way street
c approaching a junction
d going up a long hill
e the view ahead is blocked

Question 4.47

Mark one answer
You have just gone through deep water.
To dry off the brakes you should

a accelerate and keep to a high speed
   for a short time
b go slowly while gently applying the
   brakes
c avoid using the brakes at all for a few
   miles
d stop for at least an hour to allow them
   time to dry

Answers and explanations

4.1   c Remember, therefore, to allow a bigger gap when following another vehicle.

4.2   b

4.3   d

4.4   b

4.5   a

4.6   a Motorcycles are small and difficult to see. Anything that increases your chances of being seen by other road users is a good thing.

4.7   c

4.8   a, b

4.9   b, d, e

4.10   d

4.11   b, c

4.12   d

4.13   d

4.14   d

4.15   d

4.16   b, d

4.17   b, e

4.18   b

4.19   d

4.20   a

4.21   b

4.22   a, b

4.23   a

4.24   a, b, d, f

4.25   a, b

4.26   a

4.27   d

4.28   d

4.29   d Rain after a long dry spell will cause any oil or diesel to float to the surface.

4.30   d

4.31   a

4.32   c

4.33   b

4.34   a

4.35   c, d

4.36   d

4.37   d

4.38   b, c

4.39   b

4.40   d In windy conditions cyclists are all too easily blown about and may wobble or steer off course.

4.41   d

4.42   c

4.43   b

4.44   a You can see further round the bend earlier if you keep to the left.

4.45   b, c

4.46   a, c, e

4.47   b

Section 5   Hazard perception

Question 5.1

Mark two answers

You get cold and wet when riding. Which TWO are likely to happen?

a   You may lose concentration
b   You may slide off the seat
c   Your visor may freeze up
d   Your reaction times may be slower
e   Your helmet may loosen

Question 5.2

Mark one answer

You are riding up to a zebra crossing. You intend to stop for waiting pedestrians. How could you let them know you are stopping?

a   By signalling with your left arm
b   By waving them across
c   By flashing your headlight
d   By signalling with your right arm

Question 5.3

Mark one answer

You are about to ride home. You cannot find the glasses you need to wear. You should

a   ride home slowly, keeping to quiet roads
b   borrow a friend's glasses and use those
c   ride home at night, so that the lights will help you
d   find a way of getting home without riding

Question 5.4

Mark three answers

Which THREE of these are likely effects of drinking alcohol?

a   Reduced co-ordination
b   Increased confidence
c   Poor judgement
d   Increased concentration
e   Faster reactions
f   Colour blindness

Question 5.5

Mark one answer
You find that you need glasses to read vehicle number plates at the required distance. When MUST you wear them?

a   Only in bad weather conditions
b   At all times when riding
c   Only when you think it necessary
d   Only in bad light or at night time

Question 5.6

Mark three answers
Drinking any amount of alcohol is likely to

a   slow down your reactions to hazards
b   increase the speed of your reactions
c   worsen your judgement of speed
d   improve your awareness of danger
e   give a false sense of confidence

Question 5.7

Mark one answer
Which of the following types of glasses should NOT be worn when riding at night?

a   Half-moon
b   Round
c   Bi-focal
d   Tinted

Question 5.8

Mark two answers
You are not sure if your cough medicine will affect you. What TWO things could you do?

a   Ask your doctor
b   Check the medicine label
c   Ride if you feel alright
d   Ask a friend or relative for advice

Question 5.9

Mark one answer
For which of these may you use hazard warning lights?

a   When riding on a motorway to warn traffic behind of a hazard ahead
b   When you are double parked on a two-way road
c   When your direction indicators are not working
d   When warning oncoming traffic that you intend to stop

Question 5.10

When should you use hazard warning lights?

a When you are double parked on a two-way road
b When your direction indicators are not working
c When warning oncoming traffic that you intend to stop
d When your motorcycle has broken down and is causing an obstruction

Question 5.11

The road is wet. You are passing a line of queuing traffic and riding on the painted road markings. You should take extra care, particularly when

a signalling
b braking
c carrying a pillion
d checking your mirrors

Question 5.12

When riding how can you help to reduce the risk of hearing damage?

a Wearing goggles
b Using ear plugs
c Wearing a scarf
d Keeping the visor up

Question 5.13

You see this road marking in between queuing traffic. What should you look out for?

a Overhanging trees
b Road works
c Traffic wardens
d Traffic emerging

Question 5.14

Mark one answer
It is a very hot day. What would you
expect to find?

a   Mud on the road
b   A soft road surface
c   Road works ahead
d   Banks of fog

Question 5.15

Mark one answer
When riding long distances at speed,
noise can cause fatigue. What can you
do to help reduce this?

a   Vary your speed
b   Wear ear plugs
c   Use an open-face helmet
d   Ride in an upright position

Question 5.16

Mark one answer
Why should you wear ear plugs when
riding a motorcycle?

a   To help to prevent ear damage
b   To make you less aware of traffic
c   To help to keep you warm
d   To make your helmet fit better

Question 5.17

Mark one answer
You are going out to a social event and
alcohol will be available. You will be
riding your motorcycle shortly afterwards.
What is the safest thing to do?

a   Stay just below the legal limit
b   Have soft drinks and alcohol in turn
c   Don't go beyond the legal limit
d   Stick to non-alcoholic drinks

Question 5.18

Mark one answer
You are convicted of riding after drinking
too much alcohol. How could this affect
your insurance?

a   Your insurance may become invalid
b   The amount of excess you pay will be
    reduced
c   You will only be able to get third party
    cover
d   Cover will only be given for riding
    smaller motorcycles

Question 5.19

Why should you check over your shoulder before turning right into a side road?

a   To make sure the side road is clear
b   To check for emerging traffic
c   To check for overtaking vehicles
d   To confirm your intention to turn

Question 5.20

You see this sign on the rear of a slow-moving lorry that you want to pass.
It is travelling in the middle lane of a three-lane motorway. You should

a   cautiously approach the lorry then pass on either side
b   follow the lorry until you can leave the motorway
c   wait on the hard shoulder until the lorry has stopped
d   approach with care and keep to the left of the lorry

Question 5.21

Where would you expect to see these markers?

a   On a motorway sign
b   At the entrance to a narrow bridge
c   On a large goods vehicle
d   On a builder's skip placed on the road

Question 5.22

What does this signal from a police officer mean to oncoming traffic?

a   Go ahead
b   Stop
c   Turn left
d   Turn right

Question 5.23

Mark one answer
What is the main hazard shown in this picture?

a   Vehicles turning right
b   Vehicles doing U-turns
c   The cyclist crossing the road
d   Parked cars around the corner

Question 5.24

Mark one answer
Which road user has caused a hazard?

B   D   C   A

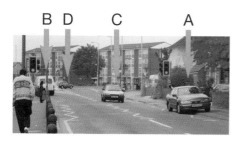

a   The parked car (arrowed A)
b   The pedestrian waiting to cross (arrowed B)
c   The moving car (arrowed C)
d   The car turning (arrowed D)

Question 5.25

Mark one answer
What should the driver of the car approaching the crossing do?

a   Continue at the same speed
b   Sound the horn
c   Drive through quickly
d   Slow down and get ready to stop

Question 5.26

Mark one answer
You think the driver of the vehicle in front has forgotten to cancel the right indicator. You should

a   flash your lights to alert the driver
b   sound your horn before overtaking
c   overtake on the left if there is room
d   stay behind and not overtake

Question 5.27

Mark three answers
What THREE things should the driver of the grey car (arrowed) be especially aware of?

a Pedestrians stepping out between cars
b Other cars behind the grey car
c Doors opening on parked cars
d The bumpy road surface
e Cars leaving parking spaces
f Empty parking spaces

Question 5.28

Mark one answer
What is the main hazard the driver of the red car (arrowed) should be most aware of?

a Glare from the sun may affect the driver's vision
b The black car may stop suddenly
c The bus may move out into the road
d Oncoming vehicles will assume the driver is turning right

Question 5.29

Mark one answer
You see this sign ahead. You should expect the road to

a go steeply uphill
b go steeply downhill
c bend sharply to the left
d bend sharply to the right

70

Question 5.30

Mark one answer

In heavy motorway traffic you are being followed closely by the vehicle behind. How can you lower the risk of an accident?

a   Increase your distance from the vehicle in front
b   Tap your foot on the brake pedal sharply
c   Switch on your hazard lights
d   Move onto the hard shoulder and stop

Question 5.31

Mark one answer

You are approaching this cyclist. You should

a   overtake before the cyclist gets to the junction
b   flash your headlights at the cyclist
c   slow down and allow the cyclist to turn
d   overtake the cyclist on the left-hand side

Question 5.32

Mark one answer

Why must you take extra care when turning right at this junction?

a   Road surface is poor
b   Footpaths are narrow
c   Road markings are faint
d   There is reduced visibility

Question 5.33

This yellow sign on a vehicle indicates this is

a   a vehicle broken down
b   a school bus
c   an ice cream van
d   a private ambulance

Question 5.34

When approaching this bridge you should give way to

a   bicycles
b   buses
c   motorcycles
d   cars

Question 5.35

What type of vehicle could you expect to meet in the middle of the road?

a   Lorry
b   Bicycle
c   Car
d   Motorcycle

Question 5.36

At this blind junction you must stop

a   behind the line, then edge forward
    to see clearly
b   beyond the line at a point where you
    can see clearly
c   only if there is traffic on the main road
d   only if you are turning to the right

Question 5.37

Mark one answer

A driver pulls out of a side road in front of you. You have to brake hard. You should

a   ignore the error and stay calm
b   flash your lights to show your annoyance
c   sound your horn to show your annoyance
d   overtake as soon as possible

Question 5.38

Mark one answer

An elderly person's driving ability could be affected because they may be unable to

a   obtain car insurance
b   understand road signs
c   react very quickly
d   give signals correctly

Question 5.39

Mark one answer

You have just passed these warning lights. What hazard would you expect to see next?

a   A level crossing with no barrier
b   An ambulance station
c   A school crossing patrol
d   An opening bridge

Question 5.40

Mark two answers

Why should you be especially cautious when going past this bus?

a   There is traffic approaching in the distance
b   The driver may open the door
c   It may suddenly move off
d   People may cross the road in front of it
e   There are bicycles parked on the pavement

Question 5.41

Mark one answer

In areas where there are 'traffic calming' measures you should

a   drive at a reduced speed
b   always drive at the speed limit
c   position in the centre of the road
d   only slow down if pedestrians are near

Question 5.42

You are planning a long journey. Do you need to plan rest stops?

a   Yes, you should plan to stop every half an hour
b   Yes, regular stops help concentration
c   No, you will be less tired if you get there as soon as possible
d   No, only fuel stops will be needed

Question 5.43

The red lights are flashing. What should you do when approaching this level crossing?

a   Go through quickly
b   Go through carefully
c   Stop before the barrier
d   Switch on hazard warning lights

Question 5.44

A driver does something that upsets you. You should

a   try not to react
b   let them know how you feel
c   flash your headlights several times
d   sound your horn

Question 5.45

What are TWO main hazards you should be aware of when going along this street?

a   Glare from the sun
b   Car doors opening suddenly
c   Lack of road markings
d   The headlights on parked cars being switched on
e   Large goods vehicles
f   Children running out from between vehicles

Question 5.46

Mark one answer

What is the main hazard you should be aware of when following this cyclist?

a The cyclist may move into the left and dismount
b The cyclist may swerve out into the road
c The contents of the cyclist's carrier may fall onto the road
d The cyclist may wish to turn right at the end of the road

Question 5.47

Mark one answer

A driver's behaviour has upset you. It may help if you

a stop and take a break
b shout abusive language
c gesture to them with your hand
d follow their car, flashing the headlights

Question 5.48

Mark two answers

When approaching this hazard why should you slow down?

a Because of the bend
b Because it's hard to see to the right
c Because of approaching traffic
d Because of animals crossing
e Because of the level crossing

Question 5.49

Mark one answer

You are on a dual carriageway. Ahead you see a vehicle with an amber flashing light. What will this be?

a An ambulance
b A fire engine
c A doctor on call
d A disabled person's vehicle

Question 5.50

You are approaching crossroads.
The traffic lights have failed. What should you do?

a Brake and stop only for large vehicles
b Brake sharply to a stop before looking
c Be prepared to brake sharply to a stop
d Be prepared to stop for any traffic

Question 5.51

What should the driver of the red car (arrowed) do?

a Wave the pedestrians who are waiting to cross
b Wait for the pedestrian in the road to cross
c Quickly drive behind the pedestrian in the road
d Tell the pedestrian in the road she should not have crossed

Question 5.52

Why are destination markings painted on the road surface?

a To restrict the flow of traffic
b To warn you of oncoming traffic
c To enable you to change lanes early
d To prevent you changing lanes

Question 5.53

You are following a slower-moving vehicle on a narrow country road. There is a junction just ahead on the right. What should you do?

a Overtake after checking your mirrors and signalling
b Stay behind until you are past the junction
c Accelerate quickly to pass before the junction
d Slow down and prepare to overtake on the left

Question 5.54

Mark one answer
What should you do as you approach this overhead bridge?

a   Move out to the centre of the road before going through
b   Find another route, this is only for high vehicles
c   Be prepared to give way to large vehicles in the middle of the road
d   Move across to the right-hand side before going through

Question 5.55

Mark one answer
Why are mirrors often slightly curved (convex)?

a   They give a wider field of vision
b   They totally cover blind spots
c   They make it easier to judge the speed of following traffic
d   They make following traffic look bigger

Answers and explanations

5.1   a, d
5.2   d
5.3   d
5.4   a, b, c
5.5   b
5.6   a, c, e
5.7   d
5.8   a, b
5.9   a
5.10 d
5.11 b Road markings can reduce the traction of your tyres on the road and so diminish your brakes' effectiveness.
5.12 b
5.13 d
5.14 b
5.15 b
5.16 a
5.17 d Any alcohol will affect your balance and judgement on a motorcycle.
5.18 a
5.19 c Overtaking vehicles might not be visible in your mirrors.
5.20 d
5.21 c, d
5.22 b
5.23 c
5.24 a
5.25 d
5.26 d
5.27 a, c, e
5.28 c
5.29 c
5.30 a
5.31 c

5.32 d
5.33 b
5.34 b
5.35 a
5.36 a
5.37 a
5.38 c
5.39 c
5.40 c, d
5.41 a Road humps and rumble strips
       are examples of traffic calming
       measures. They are often found
       in residential areas and have
       been introduced to reduce the
       overall speed of traffic.
5.42 b
5.43 c
5.44 a
5.45 b, f
5.46 b
5.47 a
5.48 a, e
5.49 d
5.50 d
5.51 b
5.52 c
5.53 b
5.54 c
5.55 a

Theory Test Questions for Motorcyclists

2003–2004

Section 6   Vulnerable road users

Question 6.1

Mark one answer
You should not ride too closely behind
a lorry because

a you will breathe in the lorry's exhaust
   fumes
b wind from the lorry will slow you
   down
c drivers behind you may not be able to
   see you
d it will reduce your view ahead

Question 6.2

Mark one answer
You are riding along a main road with
many side roads. Why should you be
particularly careful?

a Gusts of wind from the side roads
   may push you off course
b Drivers coming out from side roads
   may not see you
c The road will be more slippery where
   cars have been turning
d Drivers will be travelling slowly when
   they approach a junction

Question 6.3

Mark three answers
You are riding on a country lane. You see
cattle on the road. You should

a slow down
b stop if necessary
c give plenty of room
d rev your engine
e sound your horn
f ride up close behind them

Question 6.4

Mark one answer
A learner driver has begun to emerge into
your path from a side road on the left.
You should

a be ready to slow down and stop
b let them emerge then ride close
   behind
c turn into the side road
d brake hard, then wave them out

Question 6.5

Mark one answer
The vehicle ahead is being driven by a
learner. You should

a keep calm and be patient
b ride up close behind
c put your headlight on full beam
d sound your horn and overtake

Question 6.6

Why is it vital for a rider to make a lifesaver check before turning right?

a To check for any overtaking traffic
b To confirm that they are about to turn
c To make sure the side road is clear
d To check that the rear indicator is flashing

Question 6.7

You are riding in fast-flowing traffic. The vehicle behind is following too closely. You should

a slow down gradually to increase the gap in front of you
b slow down as quickly as possible by braking
c accelerate to get away from the vehicle behind you
d apply the brakes sharply to warn the driver behind

Question 6.8

You are riding towards a zebra crossing. Waiting to cross is a person in a wheelchair. You should

a continue on your way
b wave to the person to cross
c wave to the person to wait
d be prepared to stop

Question 6.9

Why should you allow extra room when overtaking another motorcyclist on a windy day?

a The rider may turn off suddenly to get out of the wind
b The rider may be blown across in front of you
c The rider may stop suddenly
d The rider may be travelling faster than normal

Question 6.10

Mark two answers
You have stopped at a pelican crossing. A disabled person is crossing slowly in front of you. The lights have now changed to green. You should

a   allow the person to cross
b   ride in front of the person
c   ride behind the person
d   sound your horn
e   be patient
f   edge forward slowly

Question 6.11

Mark one answer
Where should you take particular care to look out for other motorcyclists and cyclists?

a   On dual carriageways
b   At junctions
c   At zebra crossings
d   On one-way streets

Question 6.12

Mark one answer
What is a main cause of accidents among young and new motorcyclists?

a   Using borrowed equipment
b   Lack of experience and judgement
c   Riding in bad weather conditions
d   Riding on country roads

Question 6.13

Mark one answer
Young motorcyclists can often be the cause of accidents due to

a   being too cautious at junctions
b   riding in the middle of their lane
c   showing off and being competitive
d   riding when the weather is poor

Question 6.14

Mark two answers
You are about to overtake horse riders. Which TWO of the following could scare the horses?

a   Sounding your horn
b   Giving arm signals
c   Riding slowly
d   Revving your engine

82

Question 6.15

Mark one answer
Which of the following is applicable to young motorcyclists?

a They are normally better than experienced riders
b They are usually less likely to have accidents
c They are often over-confident of their own ability
d They are more likely to get cheaper insurance

Question 6.16

Mark one answer
The road outside this school is marked with yellow zigzag lines. What do these lines mean?

a You may park on the lines when dropping off schoolchildren
b You may park on the lines when picking schoolchildren up
c You must not wait or park your motorcycle here at all
d You must stay with your motorcycle if you park here

Question 6.17

Mark one answer
Which sign means that there may be people walking along the road?

a   b

c   d

Question 6.18

Mark one answer
You are turning left at a junction. Pedestrians have started to cross the road. You should

a go on, giving them plenty of room
b stop and wave at them to cross
c blow your horn and proceed
d give way to them

Question 6.19

You are turning left from a main road into a side road. People are already crossing the road into which you are turning. You should

a   continue, as it is your right of way
b   signal to them to continue crossing
c   wait and allow them to cross
d   sound your horn to warn them of your presence

Question 6.20

You are at a road junction, turning into a minor road. There are pedestrians crossing the minor road. You should

a   stop and wave the pedestrians across
b   sound your horn to let the pedestrians know that you are there
c   give way to the pedestrians who are already crossing
d   carry on; the pedestrians should give way to you

Question 6.21

You are turning left into a side road. What hazards should you be especially aware of?

a   One-way street
b   Pedestrians
c   Traffic congestion
d   Parked vehicles

Question 6.22

You intend to turn right into a side road. Just before turning you should check for motorcyclists who might be

a   overtaking on your left
b   following you closely
c   emerging from the side road
d   overtaking on your right

Question 6.23

A toucan crossing is different from other crossings because

a   moped riders can use it
b   it is controlled by a traffic warden
c   it is controlled by two flashing lights
d   cyclists can use it

Question 6.24

Mark two answers
At toucan crossings

a there is no flashing amber light
b cyclists are not permitted
c there is a continuously flashing amber beacon
d pedestrians and cyclists may cross
e you only stop if someone is waiting to cross

Question 6.25

Mark one answer
What does this sign tell you?

a No cycling
b Cycle route ahead
c Route for cycles only
d End of cycle route

Question 6.26

Mark one answer
How will a school-crossing patrol signal you to stop?

a By pointing to children on the opposite pavement
b By displaying a red light
c By displaying a stop sign
d By giving you an arm signal

Question 6.27

Mark one answer
Where would you see this sign?

a In the window of a car taking children to school
b At the side of the road
c At playground areas
d On the rear of a school bus or coach

Question 6.28

Mark one answer
Which sign tells you that pedestrians may be walking in the road as there is no pavement?

a   b

c   d

Question 6.29

Mark one answer
What does this sign mean?

a   No route for pedestrians and cyclists
b   A route for pedestrians only
c   A route for cyclists only
d   A route for pedestrians and cyclists

Question 6.30

Mark one answer
You see a pedestrian with a white stick and red band. This means that the person is

a   physically disabled
b   deaf only
c   blind only
d   deaf and blind

Question 6.31

Mark one answer
You see two elderly pedestrians about to cross the road ahead. You should

a   expect them to wait for you to pass
b   speed up to get past them quickly
c   stop and wave them across the road
d   be careful, they may misjudge your speed

Question 6.32

Mark one answer
What action would you take when elderly people are crossing the road?

a   Wave them across so they know that you have seen them
b   Be patient and allow them to cross in their own time
c   Rev the engine to let them know that you are waiting
d   Tap the horn in case they are hard of hearing

Question 6.33

Mark one answer
What does this sign mean?

a   Contraflow pedal cycle lane
b   With-flow pedal cycle lane
c   Pedal cycles and buses only
d   No pedal cycles or buses

Question 6.34

Mark one answer

You are coming up to a roundabout. A cyclist is signalling to turn right. What should you do?

a   Overtake on the right
b   Give a horn warning
c   Signal the cyclist to move across
d   Give the cyclist plenty of room

Question 6.35

Mark one answer

You are approaching this roundabout and see the cyclist signal right. Why is the cyclist keeping to the left?

a   It is a quicker route for the cyclist
b   The cyclist is going to turn left instead
c   The cyclist thinks The Highway Code does not apply to bicycles
d   The cyclist is slower and more vulnerable

Question 6.36

Mark one answer

When you are overtaking a cyclist you should leave as much room as you would give to a car. What is the main reason for this?

a   The cyclist might change lanes
b   The cyclist might get off the bike
c   The cyclist might swerve
d   The cyclist might have to make a right turn

Question 6.37

Mark two answers

Which TWO should you allow extra room when overtaking?

a   Motorcycles
b   Tractors
c   Bicycles
d   Road-sweeping vehicles

Question 6.38

Mark one answer

Why should you look particularly for motorcyclists and cyclists at junctions?

a   They may want to turn into the side road
b   They may slow down to let you turn
c   They are harder to see
d   They might not see you turn

Question 6.39

Mark one answer
You are waiting to come out of a side road. Why should you watch carefully for motorcycles?

a   Motorcycles are usually faster than cars
b   Police patrols often use motorcycles
c   Motorcycles are small and hard to see
d   Motorcycles have right of way

Question 6.40

Mark one answer
In daylight, an approaching motorcyclist is using a dipped headlight. Why?

a   So that the rider can be seen more easily
b   To stop the battery overcharging
c   To improve the rider's vision
d   The rider is inviting you to proceed

Question 6.41

Mark one answer
Motorcyclists should wear bright clothing mainly because

a   they must do so by law
b   it helps keep them cool in summer
c   the colours are popular
d   drivers often do not see them

Question 6.42

Mark one answer
There is a slow-moving motorcyclist ahead of you. You are unsure what the rider is going to do. You should

a   pass on the left
b   pass on the right
c   stay behind
d   move closer

Question 6.43

Mark one answer
Motorcyclists will often look round over their right shoulder just before turning right. This is because

a   they need to listen for following traffic
b   motorcycles do not have mirrors
c   looking around helps them balance as they turn
d   they need to check for traffic in their blind area

Question 6.44

Mark three answers
At road junctions which of the following are most vulnerable?

a   Cyclists
b   Motorcyclists
c   Pedestrians
d   Car drivers
e   Lorry drivers

88

Question 6.45

Mark one answer
Motorcyclists are particularly vulnerable

a   when moving off
b   on dual carriageways
c   when approaching junctions
d   on motorways

Question 6.46

Mark one answer
An injured motorcyclist is lying unconscious in the road. You should

a   remove the safety helmet
b   seek medical assistance
c   move the person off the road
d   remove the leather jacket

Question 6.47

Mark two answers
You are approaching a roundabout. There are horses just ahead of you. You should

a   be prepared to stop
b   treat them like any other vehicle
c   give them plenty of room
d   accelerate past as quickly as possible
e   sound your horn as a warning

Question 6.48

Mark one answer
You notice horse riders in front. What should you do FIRST?

a   Pull out to the middle of the road
b   Be prepared to slow down
c   Accelerate around them
d   Signal right

Question 6.49

Mark three answers
Which THREE should you do when passing sheep on a road?

a   Allow plenty of room
b   Go very slowly
c   Pass quickly but quietly
d   Be ready to stop
e   Briefly sound your horn

Question 6.50

Mark one answer
At night you see a pedestrian wearing reflective clothing and carrying a bright red light. What does this mean?

a You are approaching roadworks
b You are approaching an organised walk
c You are approaching a slow-moving vehicle
d You are approaching an accident black spot

Question 6.51

Mark one answer
As you approach a pelican crossing the lights change to green. Elderly people are halfway across. You should

a wave them to cross as quickly as they can
b rev your engine to make them hurry
c flash your lights in case they have not heard you
d wait because they will take longer to cross

Question 6.52

Mark one answer
There are flashing amber lights under a school warning sign. What action should you take?

a Reduce speed until you are clear of the area
b Keep up your speed and sound the horn
c Increase your speed to clear the area quickly
d Wait at the lights until they change to green

Question 6.53

Mark one answer
Which of the following types of crossing can detect when people are on them?

a Pelican
b Toucan
c Zebra
d Puffin

90

Question 6.54

You are approaching this crossing.
You should

a   prepare to slow down and stop
b   stop and wave the pedestrians across
c   speed up and pass by quickly
d   drive on unless the pedestrians step
    out

Question 6.55

You see a pedestrian with a dog. The
dog has a bright orange lead and collar.
This especially warns you that the
pedestrian is

a   elderly
b   dog training
c   colour blind
d   deaf

Question 6.56

These road markings must be kept clear
to allow

W-SCHOOL KEEP CLEAR-W

a   schoolchildren to be dropped off
b   for teachers to park
c   schoolchildren to be picked up
d   a clear view of the crossing area

Question 6.57

You must not stop on these road
markings because you may obstruct

W-SCHOOL KEEP CLEAR-W

a   children's view of the crossing area
b   teachers' access to the school
c   delivery vehicles' access to the
    school
d   emergency vehicles' access to the
    school

Question 6.58

Mark one answer
The left-hand pavement is closed due to street repairs. What should you do?

a Watch out for pedestrians walking in the road
b Use your right-hand mirror more often
c Speed up to get past the road works quicker
d Position close to the left-hand kerb

Question 6.59

Mark one answer
Where would you see this sign?

a Near a school crossing
b At a playground entrance
c On a school bus
d At a 'pedestrians only' area

Question 6.60

Mark one answer
You are following a motorcyclist on an uneven road. You should

a allow less room so you can be seen in their mirrors
b overtake immediately
c allow extra room in case they swerve to avoid pot-holes
d allow the same room as normal because road surfaces do not affect motorcyclists

Question 6.61

Mark one answer
You are following two cyclists. They approach a roundabout in the left-hand lane. In which direction should you expect the cyclists to go?

a Left
b Right
c Any direction
d Straight ahead

Question 6.62

You are travelling behind a moped. You want to turn left just ahead. You should

a overtake the moped before the junction
b pull alongside the moped and stay level until just before the junction
c sound your horn as a warning and pull in front of the moped
d stay behind until the moped has passed the junction

Question 6.63

Which THREE of the following are hazards motorcyclists present in queues of traffic?

a Cutting in just in front of you
b Riding in single file
c Passing very close to you
d Riding with their headlight on dipped beam
e Filtering between the lanes

Question 6.64

You see a horse rider as you approach a roundabout. They are signalling right but keeping well to the left. You should

a proceed as normal
b keep close to them
c cut in front of them
d stay well back

Question 6.65

How would you react to drivers who appear to be inexperienced?

a Sound your horn to warn them of your presence
b Be patient and prepare for them to react more slowly
c Flash your headlights to indicate that it is safe for them to proceed
d Overtake them as soon as possible

Question 6.66

Mark one answer

You are following a learner driver who stalls at a junction. You should

a   be patient as you expect them to make mistakes

b   stay very close behind and flash your headlight

c   start to rev your engine if they take too long to restart

d   immediately steer around them and drive on

Question 6.67

Mark one answer

You are on a country road. What should you expect to see coming towards you on YOUR side of the road?

a   Motorcycles

b   Bicycles

c   Pedestrians

d   Horse riders

Question 6.68

Mark one answer

You are turning left into a side road. Pedestrians are crossing the road near the junction. You must

a   wave them on

b   sound your horn

c   switch on your hazard lights

d   wait for them to cross

Question 6.69

Mark one answer

You are following a car driven by an elderly driver. You should

a   expect the driver to drive badly

b   flash your lights and overtake

c   be aware that the driver's reactions may not be as fast as yours

d   stay very close behind but be careful

Question 6.70

Mark one answer
You are following a cyclist. You wish to turn left just ahead. You should

a overtake the cyclist before the junction
b pull alongside the cyclist and stay level until after the junction
c hold back until the cyclist has passed the junction
d go around the cyclist on the junction

Question 6.71

Mark one answer
A horse rider is in the left-hand lane approaching a roundabout. You should expect the rider to

a go in any direction
b turn right
c turn left
d go ahead

Question 6.72

Mark one answer
You have just passed your test. How can you decrease your risk of accidents on the motorway?

a By keeping up with the car in front
b By never going over 40mph
c By staying only in the left-hand lane
d By taking further training

Question 6.73

Mark one answer
Powered vehicles used by disabled people are small and hard to see. How do they give early warning when on a dual carriageway?

a They will have a flashing red light
b They will have a flashing green light
c They will have a flashing blue light
d They will have a flashing amber light

Question 6.74

Mark one answer
You should never attempt to overtake a cyclist

a just before you turn left
b on a left-hand bend
c on a one-way street
d on a dual carriageway

Question 6.75

Mark one answer

Ahead of you there is a moving vehicle with a flashing amber beacon. This means it is

a   slow moving
b   broken down
c   a doctor's car
d   a school-crossing patrol

6.1	d
6.2	b
6.3	a, b, c
6.4	a
6.5	a
6.6	a
6.7	a
6.8	d
6.9	b
6.10	a, e
6.11	b
6.12	b
6.13	c
6.14	a, d
6.15	c
6.16	c
6.17	d Red triangles give warnings, in this case of people walking along the road. 'c' is a warning of a pedestrian crossing.
6.18	d
6.19	c
6.20	c
6.21	b
6.22	d
6.23	d
6.24	a, d
6.25	b
6.26	c
6.27	d
6.28	a
6.29	d
6.30	d
6.31	d The ability to judge speed tends to deteriorate as you get older.
6.32	b
6.33	b

6.34 d

6.35 d

6.36 c 'c' is the answer required, but you should also be aware that cyclists can be unpredictable.

6.37 a, c

6.38 c

6.39 c

6.40 a

6.41 d

6.42 c

6.43 d

6.44 a, b, c

6.45 c

6.46 b

6.47 a, c

6.48 b Horses and their riders can be unpredictable so 'b' is the safest first action.

6.49 a, b, d

6.50 b

6.51 d

6.52 a

6.53 d

6.54 a

6.55 d

6.56 d You must not park on these yellow zigzag lines, not even to drop off or pick up children.

6.57 a

6.58 a Remember that pedestrians walking in the road will have their backs to you, so give them plenty of space.

6.59 c

6.60 c

6.61 c

6.62 d

6.63 a, c, e

6.64 d

6.65 b

6.66 a

6.67 c Pedestrians are the most likely to expect as country roads often have no pavements and pedestrians are advised to walk on the right so that they can see oncoming traffic on their side of the road. However, you should always expect the unexpected when riding.

6.68 d When you turn into a side road pedestrians who are already crossing have priority so you must give way.

6.69 c

6.70 c

6.71 a

6.72 d

6.73 d

6.74 a The word 'NEVER' makes 'a' correct.

6.75 a

Section 7

Other types of vehicle

Question 7.1

Mark one answer

You are riding behind a long vehicle. There is a mini-roundabout ahead. The vehicle is signalling left, but positioned to the right. You should

a sound your horn
b overtake on the left
c keep well back
d flash your headlights

Question 7.2

Mark two answers

Why should you be careful when riding on roads where electric trams operate?

a They cannot steer to avoid you
b They move quickly and quietly
c They are noisy and slow
d They can steer to avoid you
e They give off harmful exhaust fumes

Question 7.3

Mark one answer

You are going ahead and will have to cross tram lines. Why should you be especially careful?

a Tram lines are always 'live'
b Trams will be stopping here
c Pedestrians will be crossing here
d The steel rails can be slippery

Question 7.4

Mark one answer

As a motorcyclist why should you be especially careful when crossing tram lines?

a The tram lines are 'live'
b Trams may be stopping
c Pedestrians will be crossing
d The steel rails can be slippery

Question 7.5

Mark one answer

The road is wet. Why might a motorcyclist steer round drain covers on a bend?

a To avoid puncturing the tyres on the edge of the drain covers
b To prevent the motorcycle sliding on the metal drain covers
c To help judge the bend using the drain covers as marker points
d To avoid splashing pedestrians on the pavement

Question 7.6

You are about to overtake a slow-moving motorcyclist. Which one of these signs would make you take special care?

a

b

c

d

Question 7.7

You are waiting to emerge left from a minor road. A large vehicle is approaching from the right. You have time to turn, but you should wait. Why?

a The large vehicle can easily hide an overtaking vehicle

b The large vehicle can turn suddenly

c The large vehicle is difficult to steer in a straight line

d The large vehicle can easily hide vehicles from the left

Question 7.8

You are following a long vehicle. It approaches a crossroads and signals left, but moves out to the right. You should

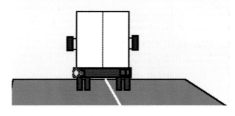

a get closer in order to pass it quickly

b stay well back and give it room

c assume the signal is wrong and it is really turning right

d overtake as it starts to slow down

Question 7.9

You are following a long vehicle approaching a crossroads. The driver signals right but moves close to the left-hand kerb. What should you do?

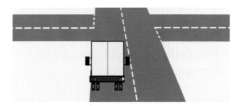

a Warn the driver of the wrong signal

b Wait behind the long vehicle

c Report the driver to the police

d Overtake on the right-hand side

Question 7.10

You are approaching a mini-roundabout. The long vehicle in front is signalling left but positioned over to the right. You should

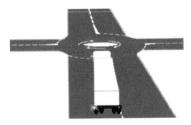

a   sound your horn
b   overtake on the left
c   follow the same course as the lorry
d   keep well back

Question 7.11

Before overtaking a large vehicle you should keep well back. Why is this?

a   To give acceleration space to overtake quickly on blind bends
b   To get the best view of the road ahead
c   To leave a gap in case the vehicle stops and rolls back
d   To offer other drivers a safe gap if they want to overtake you

Question 7.12

Why is passing a lorry more risky than passing a car?

a   Lorries are longer than cars
b   Lorries may suddenly pull up
c   The brakes of lorries are not as good
d   Lorries climb hills more slowly

Question 7.13

When you approach a bus signalling to move off from a bus stop you should

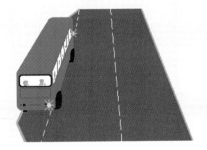

a   get past before it moves
b   allow it to pull away, if it is safe to do so
c   flash your headlights as you approach
d   signal left and wave the bus on

Question 7.14

Mark two answers
You are travelling behind a bus that pulls up at a bus stop. What should you do?

a Accelerate past the bus sounding your horn
b Watch carefully for pedestrians
c Be ready to give way to the bus
d Pull in closely behind the bus

Question 7.15

Mark one answer
You are following a large lorry on a wet road. Spray makes it difficult to see. You should

a drop back until you can see better
b put your headlights on full beam
c keep close to the lorry, away from the spray
d speed up and overtake quickly

Question 7.16

Mark one answer
Which of these vehicles is LEAST likely to be affected by crosswinds?

a Cyclists
b Motorcyclists
c High-sided vehicles
d Cars

Question 7.17

Mark one answer
Some two-way roads are divided into three lanes. Why are these particularly dangerous?

a Traffic in both directions can use the middle lane to overtake
b Traffic can travel faster in poor weather conditions
c Traffic can overtake on the left
d Traffic uses the middle lane for emergencies only

Question 7.18

What should you do as you approach this lorry?

a   Slow down and be prepared to wait
b   Make the lorry wait for you
c   Flash your light at the lorry
d   Move to the right-hand side of the road

Question 7.19

You are following a large articulated vehicle. It is going to turn left into a narrow road. What action should you take?

a   Move out and overtake on the right
b   Pass on the left as the vehicle moves out
c   Be prepared to stop behind
d   Overtake quickly before the lorry moves out

Question 7.20

You keep well back while waiting to overtake a large vehicle. A car fills the gap. You should

a   sound your horn
b   drop back further
c   flash your headlights
d   start to overtake

Question 7.21

At a junction you see this signal. It means

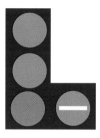

a   cars must stop
b   trams must stop
c   both trams and cars must stop
d   both trams and cars can continue

Question 7.22

Mark one answer

You are following a large vehicle approaching crossroads.The driver signals to turn left. What should you do?

a Overtake if you can leave plenty of room

b Overtake only if there are no oncoming vehicles

c Do not overtake until the vehicle begins to turn.

d Do not overtake when at or approaching a junction

Question 7.24

Mark one answer

You wish to overtake a long, slow-moving vehicle on a busy road. You should

a follow it closely and keep moving out to see the road ahead

b flash your headlights for the oncoming traffic to give way

c stay behind until the driver waves you past

d keep well back until you can see that it is clear

Question 7.23

Mark one answer

You are following a long lorry. The driver signals to turn left into a narrow road. What should you do?

a Overtake on the left before the lorry reaches the junction

b Overtake on the right as soon as the lorry slows down

c Do not overtake unless you can see there is no oncoming traffic

d Do not overtake, stay well back and be prepared to stop

Answers and explanations

7.1   c

7.2   a. b

7.3   d

7.4   d

7.5   b Water on metal is a dangerous combination, especially for a two-wheeled vehicle.

7.6   a The motorcyclist may wobble as you pass by in a windy situation.

7.7   a

7.8   b

7.9   b Long vehicles require more space to turn and often need to position for this.

7.10   d

7.11   b

7.12   a Overtaking takes time, so the longer the vehicle you overtake the greater the danger, as you will take longer to pass it.

7.13   b This helps traffic flow without giving confusing signals.

7.14   b, c

7.15   a

7.16   d Of the four mentioned, cars are by far the most stable and least affected by crosswinds.

7.17   a

7.18   a

7.19   c The large articulated vehicle may need to position to the right in order to turn left into the narrow road.

7.20   b

7.21   b

7.22   d

7.23   d

7.24   d

Theory Test Questions for Motorcyclists

2003–2004

Section 8   Motorcycle handling

Question 8.1

Mark one answer

When you are seated on a stationary motorcycle, your position should allow you to

a just touch the ground with your toes
b place both feet on the ground
c operate the centre stand
d reach the switches by stretching

Question 8.2

Mark two answers

As a safety measure before starting your engine, you should

a push the motorcycle forward to check the rear wheel turns freely
b engage first gear and apply the rear brake
c engage first gear and apply the front brake
d glance at the neutral light on your instrument panel

Question 8.3

Mark one answer

When coming to a normal stop on a motorcycle, you should

a only apply the front brake
b rely just on the rear brake
c apply both brakes smoothly
d apply either of the brakes gently

Question 8.4

Mark two answers

You are approaching this junction. As the motorcyclist you should

a prepare to slow down
b sound your horn
c keep near the left kerb
d speed up to clear the junction
e stop, as the car has right of way

Question 8.5

Mark one answer

What can you do to improve your safety on the road as a motorcyclist?

a Anticipate the actions of others
b Stay just above the speed limits
c Keep positioned close to the kerbs
d Remain well below speed limits

Question 8.6

Mark three answers

Which THREE of these can cause skidding?

a Braking too gently
b Leaning too far over when cornering
c Staying upright when cornering
d Braking too hard
e Changing direction suddenly

Question 8.7

Mark two answers

It is very cold and the road looks wet. You cannot hear any road noise. You should

a continue riding at the same speed
b ride slower in as high a gear as possible
c ride in as low a gear as possible
d keep revving your engine
e slow down as there may be black ice

Question 8.8

Mark one answer

When riding a motorcycle you should wear full protective clothing

a at all times
b only on faster, open roads
c just on long journeys
d only during bad weather

Question 8.9

Mark two answers

You have to make a journey in fog. What are the TWO most important things you should do before you set out?

a Fill up with fuel
b Make sure that you have a warm drink with you
c Check that your lights are working
d Check the battery
e Make sure that your visor is clean

Question 8.10

Mark one answer

The best place to park your motorcycle is

a on soft tarmac
b on bumpy ground
c on grass
d on firm, level ground

Question 8.11

Mark one answer

When riding in windy conditions, you should

a stay close to large vehicles
b keep your speed up
c keep your speed down
d stay close to the gutter

Question 8.12

Mark one answer
In normal riding your position on the road should be

a   about a foot from the kerb
b   about central in your lane
c   on the right of your lane
d   near the centre of the road

Question 8.13

Mark one answer
Your motorcycle is parked on a two-way road. You should get on from the

a   right and apply the rear brake
b   left and leave the brakes alone
c   left and apply the front brake
d   right and leave the brakes alone

Question 8.14

Mark one answer
To gain basic skills in how to ride a motorcycle you should

a   practise off-road with an approved training body
b   ride on the road on the first dry day
c   practise off-road in a public park or in a quiet cul-de-sac
d   ride on the road as soon as possible

Question 8.15

Mark one answer
You should not ride with your clutch lever pulled in for longer than necessary because it

a   increases wear on the gearbox
b   increases petrol consumption
c   reduces your control of the motorcycle
d   reduces the grip of the tyres

Question 8.16

Mark one answer
You are approaching a road with a surface of loose chippings. What should you do?

a   Ride normally
b   Speed up
c   Slow down
d   Stop suddenly

Question 8.17

Mark one answer
It rains after a long dry, hot spell. This may cause the road surface to

a   be unusually slippery
b   give better grip
c   become covered in grit
d   melt and break up

Question 8.18

Mark three answers

The main causes of a motorcycle skidding are

a heavy and sharp braking
b excessive acceleration
c leaning too far when cornering
d riding in wet weather
e riding in the winter

Question 8.19

Mark one answer

Riding with the side stand down could cause an accident. This is most likely to happen when

a going uphill
b accelerating
c braking
d cornering

Question 8.20

Mark one answer

To stop your motorcycle quickly in an emergency you should apply

a the rear brake only
b the front brake only
c the front brake just before the rear
d the rear brake just before the front

Question 8.21

Mark one answer

You leave the choke on for too long. This causes the engine to run too fast. When is this likely to make your motorcycle most difficult to control?

a Accelerating
b Going uphill
c Slowing down
d On motorways

Question 8.22

Mark one answer
You should NOT look down at the front wheel when riding because it can

a make your steering lighter
b improve your balance
c use less fuel
d upset your balance

Question 8.23

Mark one answer
You are entering a bend. Your side stand is not fully raised. This could

a cause an accident
b improve your balance
c alter the motorcycle's centre of gravity
d make the motorcycle more stable

Question 8.24

Mark one answer
In normal riding conditions you should brake

a by using the rear brake first and then the front
b when the motorcycle is being turned or ridden through a bend
c by pulling in the clutch before using the front brake
d when the motorcycle is upright and moving in a straight line

Question 8.25

Mark one answer
You have to brake sharply and your motorcycle starts to skid. You should

a continue braking and select a low gear
b apply the brakes harder for better grip
c select neutral and use the front brake only
d release the brakes and re-apply

Question 8.26

Mark three answers
Which THREE of the following will affect your stopping distance?

a How fast you are going
b The tyres on your motorcycle
c The time of day
d The weather
e The street lighting

Question 8.27

Mark one answer
You are on a motorway at night. You MUST have your headlights switched on unless

a there are vehicles close in front of you
b you are travelling below 50mph
c the motorway is lit
d your motorcycle is broken down on the hard shoulder

Question 8.28

Mark one answer
You have to park on the road in fog.
You should

a   leave parking lights on
b   leave no lights on
c   leave dipped headlights on
d   leave main beam headlights on

Question 8.29

Mark one answer
You ride over broken glass and get a
sudden puncture. What should you do?

a   Close the throttle and roll to a stop
b   Brake to a stop as quickly as possible
c   Release your grip on the handlebars
d   Steer from side to side to keep your
    balance

Question 8.30

Mark one answer
You see a rainbow-coloured pattern
across the road. What will this warn
you of?

a   A soft uneven road surface
b   A polished road surface
c   Fuel spilt on the road
d   Water on the road

Question 8.31

Mark one answer
You are riding in wet weather. You see
diesel fuel on the road. What should
you do?

a   Swerve to avoid the area
b   Accelerate through quickly
c   Brake sharply to a stop
d   Slow down in good time

Question 8.32

Mark one answer
Spilt fuel on the road can be very
dangerous for you as a motorcyclist.
How can this hazard be seen?

a   By a rainbow pattern on the surface
b   By a series of skid marks
c   By a pitted road surface
d   By a highly polished surface

Question 8.33

Mark one answer
Traction Control Systems (TCS) are fitted
to some motorcycles. What does this
help to prevent?

a   Wheelspin when accelerating
b   Skidding when braking too hard
c   Uneven front tyre wear
d   Uneven rear tyre wear

Question 8.34

Mark one answer

Braking too hard has caused both wheels to skid. What should you do?

a   Release both brakes together
b   Release the front then the rear brake
c   Release the front brake only
d   Release the rear brake only

Question 8.35

Mark one answer

You leave the choke on for too long. This could make the engine run faster than normal. This will make your motorcycle

a   handle much better
b   corner much safer
c   stop much more quickly
d   more difficult to control

Question 8.36

Mark four answers

Which FOUR types of road surface increase the risk of skidding for motorcyclists?

a   White lines
b   Dry tarmac
c   Tar banding
d   Yellow grid lines
e   Loose chippings

Question 8.37

Mark one answer

You are riding on a wet road. When braking you should

a   apply the rear brake well before the front
b   apply the front brake just before the rear
c   avoid using the front brake at all
d   avoid using the rear brake at all

Question 8.38

Mark one answer

You are following a vehicle at a safe distance on a wet road. Another driver overtakes you and pulls into the gap you have left. What should you do?

a   Flash your headlights as a warning
b   Try to overtake safely as soon as you can
c   Drop back to regain a safe distance
d   Stay close to the other vehicle until it moves on

Question 8.39

Mark three answers

In which THREE of these situations may you overtake another vehicle on the left?

a   When you are in a one-way street
b   When approaching a motorway slip road where you will be turning off
c   When the vehicle in front is signalling to turn right
d   When a slower vehicle is travelling in the right-hand lane of a dual carriageway
e   In slow-moving traffic queues when traffic in the right-hand lane is moving more slowly

Question 8.40

Mark one answer

You are travelling in very heavy rain. Your overall stopping distance is likely to be

a   doubled
b   halved
c   up to ten times greater
d   no different

Question 8.41

Mark one answer

When may you wait in a box junction?

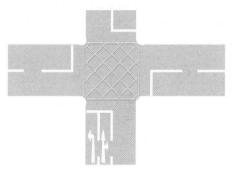

a   When you are stationary in a queue of traffic
b   When approaching a pelican crossing
c   When approaching a zebra crossing
d   When oncoming traffic prevents you turning right

Question 8.42

Mark two answers
Which TWO of the following are correct?
When overtaking at night you should

a   wait until a bend so that you can see
    the oncoming headlights
b   sound your horn twice before moving
    out
c   be careful because you can see less
d   beware of bends in the road ahead
e   put headlights on full beam

Question 8.43

Mark one answer
Which of these plates normally appear
with this road sign?

a

HumpBridge
b

Low Bridge
c

Soft Verge
d

Question 8.44

Mark three answers
Areas reserved for trams may have

a   metal studs around them
b   white line markings
c   zigzag markings
d   a different coloured surface
e   yellow hatch markings
f   a different surface texture

Question 8.45

Mark one answer
Traffic calming measures are used to

a   stop road rage
b   help overtaking
c   slow traffic down
d   help parking

Question 8.46

Mark one answer
Why should you always reduce your
speed when travelling in fog?

a   Because the brakes do not work as
    well
b   Because you could be dazzled by
    other people's fog lights
c   Because the engine is colder
d   Because it is more difficult to see
    events ahead

Question 8.47

Mark one answer
You are on a motorway in fog. The left-hand edge of the motorway can be identified by reflective studs. What colour are they?

a Green
b Amber
c Red
d White

Question 8.48

Mark two answers
A rumble device is designed to

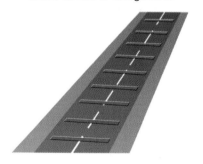

a give directions
b prevent cattle escaping
c alert you to low tyre pressure
d alert you to a hazard
e encourage you to reduce speed

Question 8.49

Mark one answer
You are on a narrow road at night. A slower-moving vehicle ahead has been signalling right for some time. What should you do?

a Overtake on the left
b Flash your headlights before overtaking
c Signal right and sound your horn
d Wait for the signal to be cancelled before overtaking

Question 8.50

Mark one answer
Why should you test your brakes after this hazard?

a Because you will be on a slippery road
b Because your brakes will be soaking wet
c Because you will have gone down a long hill
d Because you will have just crossed a long bridge

Question 8.51

Mark one answer
You have to make a journey in foggy conditions. You should

a   follow other vehicles' tail lights closely
b   avoid using dipped headlights
c   leave plenty of time for your journey
d   keep two seconds behind other vehicles

Question 8.52

Mark one answer
You are overtaking a car at night. You must be sure that

a   you flash your headlights before overtaking
b   you select a higher gear
c   you have switched your lights to full beam before overtaking
d   you do not dazzle other road users

Question 8.53

Mark one answer
You see a vehicle coming towards you on a single track road. You should

a   go back to the main road
b   do an emergency stop
c   stop at a passing place
d   put on your hazard warning lights

Question 8.54

Mark one answer
You are on a road which has speed humps. A driver in front is travelling slower than you. You should

a   sound your horn
b   overtake as soon as you can
c   flash your headlights
d   slow down and stay behind

Question 8.55

Mark one answer
You are following other vehicles in fog with your lights on. How else can you reduce the chances of being involved in an accident?

a   Keep close to the vehicle in front
b   Use your main beam instead of dipped headlights
c   Keep together with the faster vehicles
d   Reduce your speed and increase the gap

Question 8.56

Mark one answer

You see these markings on the road. Why are they there?

a To show a safe distance between vehicles

b To keep the area clear of traffic

c To make you aware of your speed

d To warn you to change direction

Question 8.57

Mark one answer

When MUST you use dipped headlights during the day?

a All the time

b Along narrow streets

c In poor visibility

d When parking

Answers and explanations

8.1   b
8.2   a, d
8.3   c In good conditions you should apply greater pressure to the front brake.
8.4   a, b
8.5   a
8.6   b, d, e
8.7   b, e
8.8   a
8.9   c, e See and be seen are the two most crucial safety aspects of driving in fog.
8.10   d
8.11   c
8.12   b Your exact position will depend on the width of the road, the road surface, your view ahead and any obstructions.
8.13   c Always mount on the side away from the traffic and apply the front brake to stop the motorcycle moving.
8.14   a
8.15   c
8.16   c
8.17   a
8.18   a, b, c
8.19   d
8.20   c
8.21   c
8.22   d
8.23   a
8.24   d
8.25   d
8.26   a, b, d

8.27   d You must use your headlights on motorways at nights even if the motorway is lit.

8.28   a

8.29   a Braking with a flat tyre can cause you to lose control of the bike.

8.30   c Fuel on the road can cause your bike to slide and lose traction.

8.31   d

8.32   a

8.33   a

8.34   a

8.35   d

8.36   a, c, d, e

8.37   b

8.38   c This may feel irritating, particularly if the circumstance is repeated several times. However, it is safest and, in reality, causes no delay.

8.39   a, c, e

8.40   a

8.41   d You may wait in a box junction if your exit is clear but oncoming traffic prevents you from turning right.

8.42   c, d

8.43   a

8.44   b, d, f

8.45   c

8.46   d Everybody knows this but an alarming number of people don't put the knowledge into practice. Accidents happen as a result.

8.47   c Red reflective studs separate the left-hand lane and the hard shoulder.

8.48   d, e A rumble device is normally raised strips or markings on the surface of the road.

8.49   d

8.50   b After driving through water your brakes will be wet, and wet brakes are inefficient.

8.51   c The Highway Code advises you to allow more time for your journey in foggy conditions. However, always ask yourself if the journey really is necessary.

8.52   d You may need to switch to full-beam headlights as you overtake, but not before.

8.53   c Bear in mind that single-track roads may have passing places at long intervals. You may meet an oncoming vehicle at a point where one of you will need to reverse to the previous nearest passing point.

8.54   d

8.55   d

8.56   c

8.57   c

Theory Test Questions for Motorcyclists

2003–2004

Section 9   Motorway rules

Question 9.1

Mark one answer
A motorcycle is not allowed on a motorway if it has an engine size smaller than

a 50cc
b 125cc
c 150cc
d 250cc

Question 9.2

Mark one answer
You are riding on a motorway. Unless signs show otherwise you must NOT exceed

a 50mph
b 60mph
c 70mph
d 80mph

Question 9.3

Mark one answer
To ride on a motorway your motorcycle must be

a 50cc or more
b 100cc or more
c 125cc or more
d 250cc or more

Question 9.4

Mark one answer
On a three-lane motorway why should you normally ride in the left lane?

a The left lane is only for lorries and motorcycles
b The left lane should only be used by smaller vehicles
c The lanes on the right are for overtaking
d Motorcycles are not allowed in the far right lane

Question 9.5

Mark one answer
You are riding at 70mph on a three-lane motorway. There is no traffic ahead. Which lane should you use?

a Any lane
b Middle lane
c Right lane
d Left lane

Question 9.6

Mark one answer
Why is it particularly important to carry out a check on your motorcycle before making a long motorway journey?

a You will have to do more harsh braking on motorways
b Motorway service stations do not deal with breakdowns
c The road surface will wear down the tyres faster
d Continuous high speeds may increase the risk of your motorcycle breaking down

Question 9.7

Mark one answer
On a motorway you may ONLY stop on the hard shoulder

a in an emergency
b if you feel tired and need to rest
c if you go past the exit that you wanted to take
d to pick up a hitchhiker

Question 9.8

Mark one answer
The emergency telephones on a motorway are connected to the

a ambulance service
b police control
c fire brigade
d breakdown service

Question 9.9

Mark one answer
You are intending to leave the motorway at the next exit. Before you reach the exit you should normally position your motorcycle

a in the middle lane
b in the left-hand lane
c on the hard shoulder
d in any lane

Question 9.10

Mark one answer
For what reason may you use the right-hand lane of a motorway?

a For keeping out of the way of lorries
b For riding at more than 70mph
c For turning right
d For overtaking other vehicles

Question 9.11

Mark one answer
You are joining a motorway from a slip road. You should

a   adjust your speed to the speed of the traffic on the motorway
b   accelerate as quickly as you can and ride straight out
c   ride onto the hard shoulder until a gap appears
d   expect drivers on the motorway to give way to you

Question 9.12

Mark four answers
Which FOUR of these must NOT use motorways?

a   Learner car drivers
b   Motorcycles over 50cc
c   Double-decker buses
d   Farm tractors
e   Horse riders
f   Cyclists

Question 9.13

Mark four answers
Which FOUR of these must NOT use motorways?

a   Learner car drivers
b   Motorcycles over 50cc
c   Double-decker buses
d   Farm tractors
e   Learner motorcyclists
f   Cyclists

Question 9.14

Mark one answer
Immediately after joining a motorway you should normally

a   try to overtake
b   re-adjust your mirrors
c   position your vehicle in the centre lane
d   keep in the left lane

Question 9.15

Mark one answer
When joining a motorway you must always

a   use the hard shoulder
b   stop at the end of the acceleration lane
c   come to a stop before joining the motorway
d   give way to traffic already on the motorway

Question 9.16

Mark one answer
What is the national speed limit for cars and motorcycles in the centre lane of a three-lane motorway?

a 40mph
b 50mph
c 60mph
d 70mph

Question 9.17

Mark one answer
What is the national speed limit on motorways for cars and motorcycles?

a 30mph
b 50mph
c 60mph
d 70mph

Question 9.18

Mark one answer
The left-hand lane on a three-lane motorway is for use by

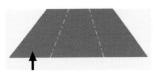

a any vehicle
b large vehicles only
c emergency vehicles only
d slow vehicles only

Question 9.19

Mark one answer
What is the right-hand lane used for on a three-lane motorway?

a Emergency vehicles only
b Overtaking
c Vehicles towing trailers
d Coaches only

Question 9.20

Mark one answer
Which of these is NOT allowed to travel in the right-hand lane of a three-lane motorway?

a A small delivery van
b A motorcycle
c A vehicle towing a trailer
d A motorcycle and side-car

Question 9.21

Mark two answers
You are travelling on a motorway. You decide you need a rest. You should

a stop on the hard shoulder
b go to a service area
c park on the slip road
d park on the central reservation
e leave at the next exit

Question 9.22 NI Exempt

Mark one answer

You break down on a motorway. You need to call for help. Why may it be better to use an emergency roadside telephone rather than a mobile phone?

a It connects you to a local garage
b Using a mobile phone will distract other drivers
c It allows easy location by the emergency services
d Mobile phones do not work on motorways

Question 9.23

Mark one answer

What should you use the hard shoulder of a motorway for?

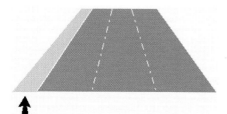

a Stopping in an emergency
b Leaving the motorway
c Stopping when you are tired
d Joining the motorway

Question 9.24

Mark one answer

After a breakdown you need to rejoin the main carriageway of a motorway from the hard shoulder. You should

a move out onto the carriageway then build up your speed
b move out onto the carriageway using your hazard lights
c gain speed on the hard shoulder before moving out onto the carriageway
d wait on the hard shoulder until someone flashes their headlights at you

Question 9.25

Mark one answer

A crawler lane on a motorway is found

a on a steep gradient
b before a service area
c before a junction
d along the hard shoulder

Question 9.26

Mark one answer
You are driving on a motorway. There are red flashing lights above every lane. You must

a pull onto the hard shoulder
b slow down and watch for further signals
c leave at the next exit
d stop and wait

Question 9.27

Mark one answer
You are driving in the right-hand lane on a motorway. You see these overhead signs. This means

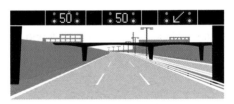

a move to the left and reduce your speed to 50mph
b there are roadworks 50 metres (55 yards) ahead
c use the hard shoulder until you have passed the hazard
d leave the motorway at the next exit

Question 9.28

Mark one answer
What do these motorway signs show?

a They are countdown markers to a bridge
b They are distance markers to the next telephone
c They are countdown markers to the next exit
d They warn of a police control ahead

Question 9.29

Mark one answer
On a motorway the amber reflective studs can be found between

a the hard shoulder and the carriageway
b the acceleration lane and the carriageway
c the central reservation and the carriageway
d each pair of the lanes

Question 9.30

Mark one answer
What colour are the reflective studs between the lanes on a motorway?

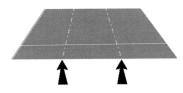

a Green
b Amber
c White
d Red

Question 9.31

Mark one answer
What colour are the reflective studs between a motorway and its slip road?

a Amber
b White
c Green
d Red

Question 9.32

Mark one answer
You are allowed to stop on a motorway when you

a need to walk and get fresh air
b wish to pick up hitch-hikers
c are told to do so by flashing red lights
d need to use a mobile telephone

Question 9.33

Mark one answer
You have broken down on a motorway. To find the nearest emergency telephone you should always walk

a with the traffic flow
b facing oncoming traffic
c in the direction shown on the marker posts
d in the direction of the nearest exit

Question 9.34

Mark one answer
You are travelling along the left lane of a three-lane motorway. Traffic is joining from a slip road. You should

a race the other vehicles
b move to another lane
c maintain a steady speed
d switch on your hazard flashers

Question 9.35

Mark one answer
You are joining a motorway. Why is it important to make full use of the slip road?

a   Because there is space available to turn round if you need to
b   To allow you direct access to the overtaking lanes
c   To build up a speed similar to traffic on the motorway
d   Because you can continue on the hard shoulder

Question 9.36

Mark one answer
How should you use the emergency telephone on a motorway?

a   Stay close to the carriageway
b   Face the oncoming traffic
c   Keep your back to the traffic
d   Stand on the hard shoulder

Question 9.37

Mark one answer
You are on a motorway. What colour are the reflective studs on the left of the carriageway?

a   Green
b   Red
c   White
d   Amber

Question 9.38

Mark one answer
On a three-lane motorway which lane should you normally use?

a   Left
b   Right
c   Centre
d   Either the right or centre

Question 9.39

Mark one answer
When going through a contraflow system on a motorway you should

a   ensure that you do not exceed 30mph
b   keep a good distance from the vehicle ahead
c   switch lanes to keep the traffic flowing
d   stay close to the vehicle ahead to reduce queues

Question 9.40

Mark one answer
A basic rule when on motorways is

a use the lane that has least traffic
b keep to the left lane unless overtaking
c overtake on the side that is clearest
d try to keep above 50mph to prevent congestion

Question 9.41

Mark one answer
You are on a three-lane motorway. There are red reflective studs on your left and white ones to your right. Where are you?

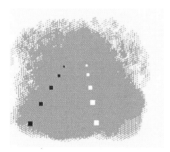

a In the right-hand lane
b In the middle lane
c On the hard shoulder
d In the left-hand lane

Question 9.42

Mark three answers
When may you stop on a motorway?

a If you have to read a map
b When you are tired and need a rest
c If red lights show above every lane
d When told to by the police
e If your mobile phone rings
f In an emergency or a breakdown

Question 9.43

Mark one answer
You are approaching roadworks on a motorway. What should you do?

a Speed up to clear the area quickly
b Always use the hard shoulder
c Obey all speed limits
d Stay very close to the vehicle in front

Question 9.44

Mark one answer

On motorways you should never overtake on the left UNLESS

a   you can see well ahead that the hard shoulder is clear

b   the traffic in the right-hand lane is signalling right

c   you warn drivers behind by signalling left

d   there is a queue of slow-moving traffic to your right that is moving slower than you are

9.1	a
9.2	c
9.3	a
9.4	c
9.5	d
9.6	d
9.7	a
9.8	b
9.9	b
9.10	d
9.11	a The slip road gives you time and space to adjust your speed to that of the traffic on the motorway.
9.12	a, d, e, f
9.13	a, d, e, f
9.14	d
9.15	d
9.16	d
9.17	d Speed limits may be altered due to weather conditions. Look out for signs on the central reserve or above your lane.
9.18	a Strictly speaking, any vehicle which is allowed on a motorway.
9.19	b
9.20	c
9.21	b, e
9.22	c
9.23	a
9.24	c
9.25	a
9.26	d
9.27	a
9.28	c
9.29	c
9.30	c

9.31　c

9.32　c

9.33　c

9.34　b

9.35　c You need to build up your speed to that of the traffic already on the motorway so you can ease into a gap in the flow of traffic.

9.36　b

9.37　b

9.38　a The other lanes should be used for overtaking.

9.39　b

9.40　b

9.41　d

9.42　c, d, f Service areas are not officially part of the motorway.

9.43　c In motorway roadworks you are sometimes, but not always, directed to use the hard shoulder, especially where the right-hand lane is closed. Therefore, 'b' is not correct. There often are lower speed limits to protect the traffic in contraflows or narrow lanes and you must obey these.

9.44　d

Section 10   Rules of the road

Question 10.1

Mark one answer
You are riding slowly in a town centre.
Before turning left you should glance
over your left shoulder to

a   check for cyclists
b   help keep your balance
c   look for traffic signs
d   check for potholes

Question 10.2

Mark two answers
As a motorcycle rider which TWO lanes
must you NOT use?

a   Crawler lane
b   Overtaking lane
c   Acceleration lane
d   Cycle lane
e   Tram lane

Question 10.3

Mark one answer
You are turning right at a large
roundabout. Just before you leave the
roundabout you should

a   take a 'lifesaver' glance over your left
    shoulder
b   take a 'lifesaver' glance over your
    right shoulder
c   put on your right indicator
d   cancel the left indicator

Question 10.4

Mark three answers
When filtering through slow-moving or
stationary traffic you should

a   watch for hidden vehicles emerging
    from side roads
b   continually use your horn as a
    warning
c   look for vehicles changing course
    suddenly
d   always ride with your hazard lights on
e   stand up on the footrests for a good
    view ahead
f   look for pedestrians walking between
    vehicles

Question 10.5

Mark one answer
You want to tow a trailer with your
motorcycle. Your engine must be more
than

a   50cc
b   125cc
c   525cc
d   1000cc

Question 10.6

Mark one answer

What is the national speed limit on a single carriageway?

a 40mph
b 50mph
c 60mph
d 70mph

Question 10.7

Mark one answer

What does this sign mean?

a No parking for solo motorcycles
b Parking for solo motorcycles
c Passing place for motorcycles
d Police motorcycles only

Question 10.8

Mark one answer

You are riding towards road works. The temporary traffic lights are at red. The road ahead is clear. What should you do?

a Ride on with extreme caution
b Ride on at normal speed
c Carry on if approaching cars have stopped
d Wait for the green light

Question 10.9

Mark one answer

You are riding on a busy dual carriageway. When changing lanes you should

a rely totally on mirrors
b always increase your speed
c signal so others will give way
d use mirrors and shoulder checks

Question 10.10

Mark one answer

You are looking for somewhere to park your motorcycle. The area is full EXCEPT for spaces marked 'disabled use'. You can

a use these spaces when elsewhere is full
b park if you stay with your motorcycle
c use these spaces, disabled or not
d not park there unless permitted

Question 10.11

Mark three answers

On which THREE occasions MUST you stop your motorcycle?

a When involved in an accident
b At a red traffic light
c When signalled to do so by a police officer
d At a junction with double broken white lines
e At a pelican crossing when the amber light is flashing and no pedestrians are crossing

Question 10.12

Mark one answer

You are on a road with passing places. It is only wide enough for one vehicle. There is a car coming towards you. What should you do?

a Pull into a passing place on your right
b Force the other driver to reverse
c Turn round and ride back to the main road
d Pull into a passing place on your left

Question 10.13

Mark one answer

You intend to go abroad and will be riding on the right-hand side of the road. What should you fit to your motorcycle?

a Twin headlights
b Headlight deflectors
c Tinted yellow brake lights
d Tinted red indicator lenses

Question 10.14

You are both turning right at this crossroads. It is safer to keep the car to your right so you can

a   see approaching traffic
b   keep close to the kerb
c   keep clear of following traffic
d   make oncoming vehicles stop

Question 10.15

What is the meaning of this sign?

a   Local speed limit applies
b   No waiting on the carriageway
c   National speed limit applies
d   No entry to vehicular traffic

Question 10.16

What is the national speed limit on a single carriageway road for cars and motorcycles?

a   70mph
b   60mph
c   50mph
d   30mph

Question 10.17

What is the national speed limit for cars and motorcycles on a dual carriageway?

a   30mph
b   50mph
c   60mph
d   70mph

Question 10.18

There are no speed limit signs on the road. How is a 30mph limit indicated?

a   By hazard warning lines
b   By street lighting
c   By pedestrian islands
d   By double or single yellow lines

Question 10.19

Where you see street lights but no speed limit signs the limit is usually

a 30mph
b 40mph
c 50mph
d 60mph

Question 10.20

What does this sign mean?

a Minimum speed 30mph
b End of maximum speed
c End of minimum speed
d Maximum speed 30mph

Question 10.21

There is a tractor ahead of you. You wish to overtake but you are NOT sure if it is safe to do so. You should

a follow another overtaking vehicle through
b sound your horn to the slow vehicle to pull over
c speed through but flash your lights to oncoming traffic
d not overtake if you are in doubt

Question 10.22

Which three of the following are most likely to take an unusual course at roundabouts?

a Horse riders
b Milk floats
c Delivery vans
d Long vehicles
e Estate cars
f Cyclists

Question 10.23

Mark four answers
In which FOUR places must you NOT park or wait?

a   On a dual carriageway
b   At a bus stop
c   On the slope of a hill
d   Opposite a traffic island
e   In front of someone else's drive
f   On the brow of a hill

Question 10.24

Mark two answers
In which TWO places must you NOT park?

a   Near a school entrance
b   Near a police station
c   In a side road
d   At a bus stop
e   In a one-way street

Question 10.25

Mark one answer
On a clearway you must not stop

a   at any time
b   when it is busy
c   in the rush hour
d   during daylight hours

Question 10.26

Mark one answer
What is the meaning of this sign?

a   No entry
b   Waiting restrictions
c   National speed limit
d   School crossing patrol

Question 10.27

Mark one answer
You can park on the right-hand side of a road at night

a   in a one-way street
b   with your sidelights on
c   more than 10 metres (32 feet) from a junction
d   under a lamp-post

Question 10.28

Mark one answer
On a three-lane dual carriageway the right-hand lane can be used for

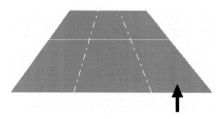

a overtaking only, never turning right
b overtaking or turning right
c fast-moving traffic only
d turning right only, never overtaking

Question 10.29

Mark one answer
You are approaching a busy junction. There are several lanes with road markings. At the last moment you realise that you are in the wrong lane. You should

a continue in that lane
b force your way across
c stop until the area has cleared
d use clear arm signals to cut across

Question 10.30

Mark one answer
Where may you overtake on a one-way street?

a Only on the left-hand side
b Overtaking is not allowed
c Only on the right-hand side
d Either on the right or the left

Question 10.31

Mark one answer
When going straight ahead at a roundabout you should

a indicate left before leaving the roundabout
b not indicate at any time
c indicate right when approaching the roundabout
d indicate left when approaching the roundabout

Question 10.32

Mark one answer
Which vehicle might have to use a different course to normal at roundabouts?

a Sports car
b Van
c Estate car
d Long vehicle

Question 10.33

Mark one answer
You are going straight ahead at a roundabout. How should you signal?

a   Signal right on the approach and then left to leave the roundabout
b   Signal left as you leave the roundabout
c   Signal left on the approach to the roundabout and keep the signal on until you leave
d   Signal left just after you pass the exit before the one you will take

Question 10.34

Mark one answer
You may only enter a box junction when

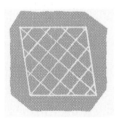

a   there are less than two vehicles in front of you
b   the traffic lights show green
c   your exit road is clear
d   you need to turn left

Question 10.35

Mark one answer
You may wait in a yellow box junction when

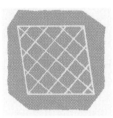

a   oncoming traffic is preventing you from turning right
b   you are in a queue of traffic turning left
c   you are in a queue of traffic to go ahead
d   you are on a roundabout

Question 10.36

Mark three answers
You MUST stop when signalled to do so by which THREE of these?

a   A police officer
b   A pedestrian
c   A school crossing patrol
d   A bus driver
e   A red traffic light

Question 10.37

Mark one answer

You will see these markers when approaching

a   the end of a motorway
b   a concealed level crossing
c   a concealed speed limit sign
d   the end of a dual carriageway

Question 10.38

Mark one answer

Someone is waiting to cross at a zebra crossing. They are standing on the pavement. You should normally

a   go on quickly before they step onto the crossing
b   stop before you reach the zigzag lines and let them cross
c   stop, let them cross, wait patiently
d   ignore them as they are still on the pavement

Question 10.39

Mark one answer

At toucan crossings, apart from pedestrians you should be aware of

a   emergency vehicles emerging
b   buses pulling out
c   trams crossing in front
d   cyclists riding across

Question 10.40

Mark two answers

Who can use a toucan crossing?

a   Trains
b   Cyclists
c   Buses
d   Pedestrians
e   Trams

Question 10.41

Mark one answer

At a pelican crossing, what does a flashing amber light mean?

a   You must not move off until the lights stop flashing
b   You must give way to pedestrians still on the crossing
c   You can move off, even if pedestrians are still on the crossing
d   You must stop because the lights are about to change to red

Question 10.42

Mark one answer

You are waiting at a pelican crossing. The red light changes to flashing amber. This means you must

a wait for pedestrians on the crossing to clear

b move off immediately without any hesitation

c wait for the green light before moving off

d get ready and go when the continuous amber light shows

Question 10.43

Mark one answer

When can you park on the left opposite these road markings?

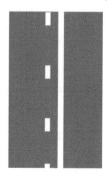

a If the line nearest to you is broken

b When there are no yellow lines

c To pick up or set down passengers

d During daylight hours only

Question 10.44

Mark one answer

You are travelling on a well-lit road at night in a built-up area. By using dipped headlights you will be able to

a see further along the road

b go at a much faster speed

c switch to main beam quickly

d be easily seen by others

Question 10.45

Mark one answer

You are intending to turn right at a crossroads. An oncoming driver is also turning right. It will normally be safer to

a keep the other vehicle to your RIGHT and turn behind it (offside to offside)

b keep the other vehicle to your LEFT and turn in front of it (nearside to nearside)

c carry on and turn at the next junction instead

d hold back and wait for the other driver to turn first

Question 10.46

Mark one answer
You are on a road that has no traffic signs. There are street lights. What is the speed limit?

a 20mph
b 30mph
c 40mph
d 60mph

Question 10.47

Mark three answers
You are going along a street with parked vehicles on the left-hand side. For which THREE reasons should you keep your speed down?

a So that oncoming traffic can see you more clearly
b You may set off car alarms
c Vehicles may be pulling out
d Drivers' doors may open
e Children may run out from between the vehicles

Question 10.48

Mark one answer
You meet an obstruction on your side of the road. You should

a carry on, you have priority
b give way to oncoming traffic
c wave oncoming vehicles through
d accelerate to get past first

Question 10.49

Mark two answers
You are on a two-lane dual carriageway. For which TWO of the following would you use the right-hand lane?

a Turning right
b Normal progress
c Staying at the minimum allowed speed
d Constant high speed
e Overtaking slower traffic
f Mending punctures

Question 10.50

Mark one answer
Who has priority at an unmarked crossroads?

a The larger vehicle
b No one has priority
c The faster vehicle
d The smaller vehicle

Question 10.51 NI Exempt

Mark one answer
What is the nearest you may park to a junction?

a   10 metres (32 feet)
b   12 metres (39 feet)
c   15 metres (49 feet)
d   20 metres (66 feet)

Question 10.52 NI Exempt

Mark three answers
In which THREE places must you NOT park?

a   Near the brow of a hill
b   At or near a bus stop
c   Where there is no pavement
d   Within 10 metres (32 feet) of a junction
e   On a 40mph road

Question 10.53

Mark one answer
You are waiting at a level crossing. A train has passed but the lights keep flashing. You must

a   carry on waiting
b   phone the signal operator
c   edge over the stop line and look for trains
d   park and investigate

Question 10.54

Mark one answer
You park overnight on a road with a 40mph speed limit. You should park

a   facing the traffic
b   with parking lights on
c   with dipped headlights on
d   near a street light

Question 10.55

Mark one answer
The dual carriageway you are turning right onto has a very narrow central reserve. What should you do?

a   Proceed to the central reserve and wait
b   Wait until the road is clear in both directions
c   Stop in the first lane so that other vehicles give way
d   Emerge slightly to show your intentions

Question 10.56

Mark one answer
At a crossroads there are no signs or road markings. Two vehicles approach. Which has priority?

a   Neither of the vehicles
b   The vehicle travelling the fastest
c   Oncoming vehicles turning right
d   Vehicles approaching from the right

145

Question 10.57

Mark one answer

What does this sign tell you?

a   That it is a no-through road
b   End of traffic calming zone
c   Free parking zone ends
d   No waiting zone ends

Question 10.58

Mark one answer

You are entering an area of roadworks. There is a temporary speed limit displayed. You should

a   not exceed the speed limit
b   obey the limit only during rush hour
c   ignore the displayed limit
d   obey the limit except at night

10.1   a
10.2   d, e
10.3   a
10.4   a, c, f
10.5   b
10.6   c
10.7   b
10.8   d
10.9   d
10.10 d
10.11 a, b, c
10.12 d
10.13 b If you do not fit deflectors you will dazzle other road users when travelling abroad.
10.14 a
10.15 c
10.16 b
10.17 d The national speed limit is 70mph on a motorway or dual carriageway and 60mph on two-way roads unless traffic signs denote anything different.
10.18 b
10.19 a
10.20 c
10.21 d
10.22 a, d, f
10.23 b, d, e, f
10.24 a, d
10.25 a
10.26 b
10.27 a
10.28 b
10.29 a All the other actions suggested could be dangerous.
10.30 d

10.31 a You should signal left just as you pass the exit before the one you want to take.

10.32 d

10.33 d This is correct for most roundabouts. Bear in mind that some roundabouts do not have an exit to the left, so the first exit is straight ahead.

10.34 c

10.35 a

10.36 a, c, e Note the word 'MUST' in the question, which is asking what the law says.

10.37 b These countdown markers indicate the distance to the stop line at the concealed level crossing.

10.38 c

10.39 d Cyclists are allowed to ride across toucan crossings, unlike other crossings where they must dismount.

10.40 b, d Toucan crossings are shared by pedestrians and cyclists together.

10.41 b

10.42 a

10.43 c

10.44 d

10.45 a

10.46 b If there are street lights, the speed limit is 30mph unless a road sign states otherwise.

10.47 c, d, e

10.48 b

10.49 a, e

10.50 b An unmarked crossroads has no road signs or road markings and no vehicle has priority even if one road is wider or busier than the other

10.51 a

10.52 a, b, d

10.53 a

10.54 b

10.55 b Because the central reserve is narrow, you would partly block the road if you drove to the middle and had to wait.

10.56 a You often find these on housing estates. Approach with caution and be prepared to give way.

10.57 d

10.58 a

Theory Test Questions for Motorcyclists

2003–2004

Section 11 Road and traffic signs

Question 11.1

Mark one answer
How should you give an arm signal to turn left?

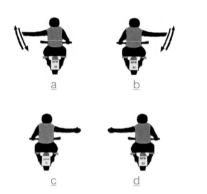

a   b

c   d

Question 11.2

Mark one answer
You are giving an arm signal ready to turn left. Why should you NOT continue with the arm signal while you turn?

a   Because you might hit a pedestrian on the corner
b   Because you will have less steering control
c   Because you will need to keep the clutch applied
d   Because other motorists will think that you are stopping on the corner

Question 11.3

Mark one answer
This sign is of particular importance to motorcyclists. It means

a   side winds
b   airport
c   slippery road
d   service area

Question 11.4

Mark one answer
Which one of these signs are you allowed to ride past on a solo motorcycle?

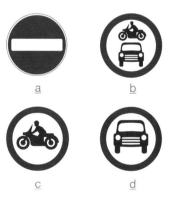

a   b

c   d

Question 11.5

Mark one answer
Which of these signals should you give when slowing or stopping your motorcycle?

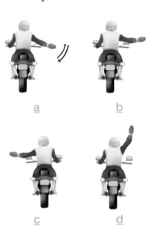

a   b

c   d

Question 11.6

Mark one answer
You are riding on a motorway. There is a slow-moving vehicle ahead. On the back you see this sign. What should you do?

a   Pass on the right
b   Pass on the left
c   Leave at the next exit
d   Drive no further

Question 11.7

Mark one answer
When drivers flash their headlights at you it means

a   that there is a radar speed trap ahead
b   that they are giving way to you
c   that they are warning you of their presence
d   that there is something wrong with your motorcycle

Question 11.8

Mark one answer
Why should you make sure that you cancel your indicators after turning?

a   To avoid flattening the battery
b   To avoid misleading other road users
c   To avoid dazzling other road users
d   To avoid damage to the indicator relay

Question 11.9

Mark one answer
Your indicators are difficult to see due to bright sunshine. When using them you should

a   also give an arm signal
b   sound your horn
c   flash your headlight
d   keep both hands on the handlebars

Question 11.10

Mark one answer
You MUST obey signs giving orders.
These signs are mostly in

a   green rectangles
b   red triangles
c   blue rectangles
d   red circles

Question 11.11

Mark one answer
Traffic signs giving orders are generally
which shape?

a   b   c   d

Question 11.12

Mark one answer
Which type of sign tells you NOT to do
something?

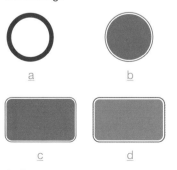

a   b

c   d

Question 11.13

Mark one answer
What does this sign mean?

a   Maximum speed limit with traffic
    calming
b   Minimum speed limit with traffic
    calming
c   '20 cars only' parking zone
d   Only 20 cars allowed at any one time

Question 11.14

Mark one answer
Which sign means no motor vehicles are
allowed?

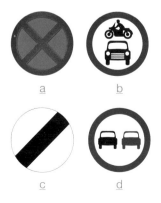

a   b

c   d

Question 11.15

Mark one answer
Which of these signs means no motor vehicles?

a

b

c

d

Question 11.16

Mark one answer
What does this sign mean?

a New speed limit 20mph
b No vehicles over 30 tonnes
c Minimum speed limit 30mph
d End of 20mph zone

Question 11.17

Mark one answer
What does this sign mean?

a No overtaking
b No motor vehicles
c Clearway (no stopping)
d Cars and motorcycles only

Question 11.18

Mark one answer
What does this sign mean?

a No parking
b No road markings
c No through road
d No entry

Question 11.19

What does this sign mean?

a Bend to the right
b Road on the right closed
c No traffic from the right
d No right turn

Question 11.20

Which sign means 'no entry'?

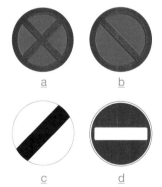

a

b

c

d

Question 11.21

What does this sign mean?

a Route for trams only
b Route for buses only
c Parking for buses only
d Parking for trams only

Question 11.22

Which type of vehicle does this sign apply to?

a Wide vehicles
b Long vehicles
c High vehicles
d Heavy vehicles

Question 11.23

Mark one answer
Which sign means NO motor vehicles allowed?

a

b

c

d

Question 11.24

Mark one answer
What does this sign mean?

a You have priority
b No motor vehicles
c Two-way traffic
d No overtaking

Question 11.25

Mark one answer
What does this sign mean?

a Keep in one lane
b Give way to oncoming traffic
c Do not overtake
d Form two lanes

Question 11.26

Mark one answer
Which sign means no overtaking?

a

b

c

d

Question 11.27

Mark one answer
What does this sign mean?

a   Waiting restrictions apply
b   Waiting permitted
c   National speed limit applies
d   Clearway (no stopping)

Question 11.28

Mark one answer
What does this sign mean?

a   End of restricted speed area
b   End of restricted parking area
c   End of clearway
d   End of cycle route

Question 11.29

Mark one answer
Which sign means 'no stopping'?

a   b

c   d

Question 11.30

Mark one answer
What does this sign mean?

a   Roundabout
b   Crossroads
c   No stopping
d   No entry

Question 11.31

Mark one answer
You see this sign ahead. It means

a national speed limit applies
b waiting restrictions apply
c no stopping
d no entry

Question 11.32

Mark one answer
What does this sign mean?

a Distance to parking place ahead
b Distance to public telephone ahead
c Distance to public house ahead
d Distance to passing place ahead

Question 11.33

Mark one answer
What does this sign mean?

a Vehicles may not park on the verge or footway
b Vehicles may park on the left-hand side of the road only
c Vehicles may park fully on the verge or footway
d Vehicles may park on the right-hand side of the road only

Question 11.34

Mark one answer
What does this traffic sign mean?

a No overtaking allowed
b Give priority to oncoming traffic
c Two-way traffic
d One-way traffic only

Question 11.35

Mark one answer
What is the meaning of this traffic sign?

a   End of two-way road
b   Give priority to vehicles coming towards you
c   You have priority over vehicles coming towards you
d   Bus lane ahead

Question 11.36

Mark one answer
What MUST you do when you see this sign?

a   Stop, ONLY if traffic is approaching
b   Stop, even if the road is clear
c   Stop, ONLY if children are waiting to cross
d   Stop, ONLY if a red light is showing

Question 11.37

Mark one answer
What does this sign mean?

a   No overtaking
b   You are entering a one-way street
c   Two-way traffic ahead
d   You have priority over vehicles from the opposite direction

Question 11.38

Mark one answer
What shape is a STOP sign at a junction?

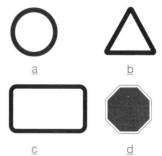

a   b

c   d

Question 11.39

Mark one answer

At a junction you see this sign partly covered by snow. What does it mean?

a Crossroads
b Give way
c Stop
d Turn right

Question 11.40

Mark one answer

Which shape is used for a GIVE WAY sign?

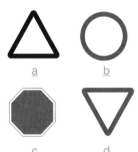

a

b

c

d

Question 11.41

Mark one answer

What does this sign mean?

a Service area 30 miles ahead
b Maximum speed 30mph
c Minimum speed 30mph
d Lay-by 30 miles ahead

Question 11.42

Mark one answer

Which of these signs means turn left ahead?

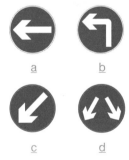

a

b

c

d

Question 11.43

Mark one answer
What does this sign mean?

a   Buses turning
b   Ring road
c   Mini roundabout
d   Keep right

Question 11.44

Mark one answer
What does this sign mean?

a   Give way to oncoming vehicles
b   Approaching traffic passes you on both sides
c   Turn off at the next available junction
d   Pass either side to get to the same destination

Question 11.45

Mark one answer
What does this sign mean?

a   Route for trams
b   Give way to trams
c   Route for buses
d   Give way to buses

Question 11.46

Mark one answer
What does a circular traffic sign with a blue background do?

a   Give warning of a motorway ahead
b   Give directions to a car park
c   Give motorway information
d   Give an instruction

Question 11.47

Mark one answer
Which of these signs means that you are entering a one-way street?

a

b

c

d

Question 11.48

Mark one answer
Where would you see a contraflow bus and cycle lane?

a   On a dual carriageway
b   On a roundabout
c   On an urban motorway
d   On a one-way street

Question 11.49

Mark one answer
What does this sign mean?

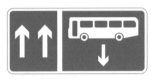

a   Bus station on the right
b   Contraflow bus lane
c   With-flow bus lane
d   Give way to buses

Question 11.50

Mark one answer
What does this sign mean?

a   With-flow bus and cycle lane
b   Contraflow bus and cycle lane
c   No buses and cycles allowed
d   No waiting for buses and cycles

161

Question 11.51

What does a sign with a brown
background show?

a Tourist directions
b Primary roads
c Motorway routes
d Minor routes

Question 11.52

This sign means

a tourist attraction
b beware of trains
c level crossing
d beware of trams

Question 11.53

What are triangular signs for?

a To give warnings
b To give information
c To give orders
d To give directions

Question 11.54

What does this sign mean?

a Turn left ahead
b T-junction
c No through road
d Give way

Question 11.55

Mark one answer
What does this sign mean?

a   Multi-exit roundabout
b   Risk of ice
c   Six roads converge
d   Place of historical interest

Question 11.56

Mark one answer
What does this sign mean?

a   Crossroads
b   Level crossing with gate
c   Level crossing without gate
d   Ahead only

Question 11.57

Mark one answer
What does this sign mean?

a   Ring road
b   Mini-roundabout
c   No vehicles
d   Roundabout

Question 11.58

Mark four answers
Which FOUR of these would be indicated by a triangular road sign?

a   Road narrows
b   Ahead only
c   Low bridge
d   Minimum speed
e   Children crossing
f   T-junction

Question 11.59

Mark one answer
What does this sign mean?

a   Cyclists must dismount
b   Cycles are not allowed
c   Cycle route ahead
d   Cycle in single file

Question 11.60

Mark one answer
Which sign means that pedestrians may be walking along the road?

a   b

c   d

Question 11.61

Mark one answer
Which of these signs warn you of a pedestrian crossing?

a   b

c   d

Question 11.62

Mark one answer
What does this sign mean?

a   No footpath ahead
b   Pedestrians only ahead
c   Pedestrian crossing ahead
d   School crossing ahead

Question 11.63

Mark one answer
What does this sign mean?

a   School crossing patrol
b   No pedestrians allowed
c   Pedestrian zone – no vehicles
d   Pedestrian crossing ahead

Question 11.64

Mark one answer
Which of these signs means there is a double bend ahead?

Question 11.65

Mark one answer
What does this sign mean?

a   Wait at the barriers
b   Wait at the crossroads
c   Give way to trams
d   Give way to farm vehicles

Question 11.66

Mark one answer
What does this sign mean?

a   Humpback bridge
b   Humps in the road
c   Entrance to tunnel
d   Soft verges

165

Question 11.67

Mark one answer
What does this sign mean?

a Low bridge ahead
b Tunnel ahead
c Ancient monument ahead
d Accident black spot ahead

Question 11.68

Mark one answer
What does this sign mean?

a Two-way traffic straight ahead
b Two-way traffic crossing a one-way street
c Two-way traffic over a bridge
d Two-way traffic crosses a two-way road

Question 11.69

Mark one answer
Which sign means 'two-way traffic crosses a one-way road'?

a

b

c

d

Question 11.70

Mark one answer
Which of these signs means the end of a dual carriageway?

a

b

c

d

Question 11.71

Mark one answer
What does this sign mean?

a   End of dual carriageway
b   Tall bridge
c   Road narrows
d   End of narrow bridge

Question 11.72

Mark one answer
What does this sign mean?

a   Two-way traffic ahead across a one-way street
b   Traffic approaching you has priority
c   Two-way traffic straight ahead
d   Motorway contraflow system ahead

Question 11.73

Mark one answer
What does this sign mean?

a   Crosswinds
b   Road noise
c   Airport
d   Adverse camber

Question 11.74

Mark one answer
What does this traffic sign mean?

a   Slippery road ahead
b   Tyres liable to punctures ahead
c   Danger ahead
d   Service area ahead

Question 11.75

Mark one answer
You are about to overtake when you see this sign. You should

a overtake the other driver as quickly as possible
b move to the right to get a better view
c switch your headlights on before overtaking
d hold back until you can see clearly ahead

Question 11.76

Mark one answer
What does this sign mean?

a Level crossing with gate or barrier
b Gated road ahead
c Level crossing without gate or barrier
d Cattle grid ahead

Question 11.77

Mark one answer
What does this sign mean?

a No trams ahead
b Oncoming trams
c Trams crossing ahead
d Trams only

Question 11.78

Mark one answer
What does this sign mean?

a Adverse camber
b Steep hill downwards
c Uneven road
d Steep hill upwards

Question 11.79

Mark one answer
What does this sign mean?

a Uneven road surface
b Bridge over the road
c Road ahead ends
d Water across the road

Question 11.80

Mark one answer
What does this sign mean?

a Humpback bridge
b Traffic calming hump
c Low bridge
d Uneven road

Question 11.81

Mark one answer
What does this sign mean?

a Turn left for parking area
b No through road on the left
c No entry for traffic turning left
d Turn left for ferry terminal

Question 11.82

Mark one answer
What does this sign mean?

a T-junction
b No through road
c Telephone box ahead
d Toilet ahead

Question 11.83

Which sign means 'no through road'?

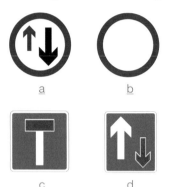

a   b

c   d

Question 11.84

Which of the following signs informs you that you are coming to a No Through Road?

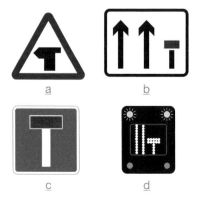

a   b

c   d

Question 11.85

What does this sign mean?

a Direction to park and ride car park
b No parking for buses or coaches
c Directions to bus and coach park
d Parking area for cars and coaches

Question 11.86

You are driving through a tunnel and you see this sign. What does it mean?

a Direction to emergency pedestrian exit
b Beware of pedestrians, no footpath ahead
c No access for pedestrians
d Beware of pedestrians crossing ahead

Question 11.87

Mark one answer
Which is the sign for a ring road?

a

b

c

d

Question 11.88

Mark one answer
What does this sign mean?

a Route for lorries
b Ring road
c Rest area
d Roundabout

Question 11.89

Mark one answer
What does this sign mean?

a Hilly road
b Humps in road
c Holiday route
d Hospital route

Question 11.90

Mark one answer
What does this sign mean?

a The right-hand lane ahead is narrow
b Right-hand lane for buses only
c Right-hand lane for turning right
d The right-hand lane is closed

Question 11.91

Mark one answer
What does this sign mean?

a Change to the left lane
b Leave at the next exit
c Contraflow system
d One-way street

Question 11.93

Mark one answer
What does this sign mean?

a Leave motorway at next exit
b Lane for heavy and slow vehicles
c All lorries use the hard shoulder
d Rest area for lorries

Question 11.92

Mark three answers
To avoid an accident when entering a contraflow system, you should

a reduce speed in good time
b switch lanes anytime to make progress
c choose an appropriate lane early
d keep the correct separation distance
e increase speed to pass through quickly
f follow other motorists closely to avoid long queues

Question 11.94

Mark one answer
You are approaching a red traffic light. The signal will change from red to

a red and amber, then green
b green, then amber
c amber, then green
d green and amber, then green

Question 11.95

Mark one answer
A red traffic light means

a   you should stop unless turning left

b   stop, if you are able to brake safely

c   you must stop and wait behind the stop line

d   proceed with caution

Question 11.96

Mark one answer
At traffic lights, amber on its own means

a   prepare to go

b   go if the way is clear

c   go if no pedestrians are crossing

d   stop at the stop line

Question 11.97

Mark one answer
You are approaching traffic lights. Red and amber are showing. This means

a   pass the lights if the road is clear

b   there is a fault with the lights – take care

c   wait for the green light before you pass the lights

d   the lights are about to change to red

Question 11.98

Mark one answer
You are at a junction controlled by traffic lights. When should you NOT proceed at green?

a   When pedestrians are waiting to cross

b   When your exit from the junction is blocked

c   When you think the lights may be about to change

d   When you intend to turn right

Question 11.99

Mark one answer
Mark one answer
You are in the left-hand lane at traffic lights. You are waiting to turn left. At which of these traffic lights must you NOT move on?

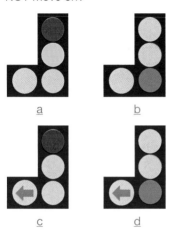

a   b

c   d

Question 11.100

Mark one answer
What does this sign mean?

a   Traffic lights out of order
b   Amber signal out of order
c   Temporary traffic lights ahead
d   New traffic lights ahead

Question 11.101

Mark one answer
When traffic lights are out of order, who has priority?

a   Traffic going straight on
b   Traffic turning right
c   Nobody
d   Traffic turning left

Question 11.102

Mark three answers
These flashing red lights mean STOP. In which THREE of the following places could you find them?

a   Pelican crossings
b   Lifting bridges
c   Zebra crossings
d   Level crossings
e   Motorway exits
f   Fire stations

Question 11.103

Mark one answer
What do these zigzag lines at pedestrian crossings mean?

a No parking at any time
b Parking allowed only for a short time
c Slow down to 20mph
d Sounding horns is not allowed

Question 11.104

Mark one answer
When may you cross a double solid white line in the middle of the road?

a To pass traffic that is queuing back at a junction
b To pass a car signalling to turn left ahead
c To pass a road maintenance vehicle travelling at 10mph or less
d To pass a vehicle that is towing a trailer

Question 11.105

Mark one answer
What does this road marking mean?

a Do not cross the line
b No stopping allowed
c You are approaching a hazard
d No overtaking allowed

Question 11.106

Mark one answer
This marking appears on the road just before a

a no entry sign
b give way sign
c stop sign
d no through road sign

Question 11.107

Mark one answer
Where would you see this road marking?

a   At traffic lights
b   On road humps
c   Near a level crossing
d   At a box junction

Question 11.108

Mark one answer
Which is a hazard warning line?

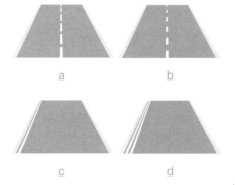

Question 11.109

Mark one answer
At this junction there is a stop sign with a solid white line on the road surface. Why is there a stop sign here?

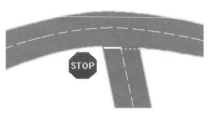

a   Speed on the major road is de-restricted
b   It is a busy junction
c   Visibility along the major road is restricted
d   There are hazard warning lines in the centre of the road

Question 11.110

Mark one answer
You see this line across the road at the entrance to a roundabout. What does it mean?

a   Give way to traffic from the right
b   Traffic from the left has right of way
c   You have right of way
d   Stop at the line

Question 11.111

Mark one answer
Where would you find this road marking?

a At a railway crossing
b At a junction
c On a motorway
d On a pedestrian crossing

Question 11.112

Mark one answer
How will a police officer in a patrol vehicle normally get you to stop?

a Flash the headlights, indicate left and point to the left
b Wait until you stop, then approach you
c Use the siren, overtake, cut in front and stop
d Pull alongside you, use the siren and wave you to stop

Question 11.113

Mark one answer
There is a police car following you. The police officer flashes the headlights and points to the left. What should you do?

a Turn at the next left
b Pull up on the left
c Stop immediately
d Move over to the left

Question 11.114

Mark one answer
You approach a junction. The traffic lights are not working. A police officer gives this signal. You should

a turn left only
b turn right only
c stop level with the officer's arm
d stop at the stop line

Question 11.115

Mark one answer
The driver of the car in front is giving this arm signal. What does it mean?

a   The driver is slowing down
b   The driver intends to turn right
c   The driver wishes to overtake
d   The driver intends to turn left

Question 11.116

Mark one answer
Where would you see these road markings?

a   At a level crossing
b   On a motorway slip road
c   At a pedestrian crossing
d   On a single-track road

Question 11.117

Mark one answer
When may you NOT overtake on the left?

a   On a free-flowing motorway or dual carriageway
b   When the traffic is moving slowly in queues
c   On a one-way street
d   When the car in front is signalling to turn right

Question 11.118

Mark one answer
What does this motorway sign mean?

a   Change to the lane on your left
b   Leave the motorway at the next exit
c   Change to the opposite carriageway
d   Pull up on the hard shoulder

Question 11.119

Mark one answer

What does this motorway sign mean?

a Temporary minimum speed 50mph

b No services for 50 miles

c Obstruction 50 metres (164 feet) ahead

d Temporary maximum speed 50mph

Question 11.120

Mark one answer

What does this sign mean?

a Through traffic to use left lane

b Right-hand lane T-junction only

c Right-hand lane closed ahead

d 11 tonne weight limit

Question 11.121

Mark one answer

On a motorway this sign means

a move over onto the hard shoulder

b overtaking on the left only

c leave the motorway at the next exit

d move to the lane on your left

Question 11.122

Mark one answer

What does '25' mean on this motorway sign?

a The distance to the nearest town

b The route number of the road

c The number of the next junction

d The speed limit on the slip road

Question 11.123

Mark one answer
The right-hand lane of a three-lane motorway is

a   for lorries only
b   an overtaking lane
c   the right-turn lane
d   an acceleration lane

Question 11.124

Mark one answer
Where can you find reflective amber studs on a motorway?

a   Separating the slip road from the motorway
b   On the left-hand edge of the road
c   On the right-hand edge of the road
d   Separating the lanes

Question 11.125

Mark one answer
Where on a motorway would you find green reflective studs?

a   Separating driving lanes
b   Between the hard shoulder and the carriageway
c   At slip road entrances and exits
d   Between the carriageway and the central reservation

Question 11.126

Mark one answer
You are travelling along a motorway. You see this sign. You should

a   leave the motorway at the next exit
b   turn left immediately
c   change lane
d   move onto the hard shoulder

Question 11.127

Mark one answer
What does this sign mean?

a   No motor vehicles
b   End of motorway
c   No through road
d   End of bus lane

Question 11.128

Mark one answer
Which of these signs means that the national speed limit applies?

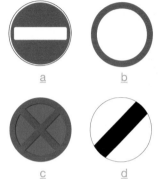

a   b

c   d

Question 11.129

Mark one answer
What is the maximum speed on a single carriageway road?

a   50mph
b   60mph
c   40mph
d   70mph

Question 11.130

Mark one answer
What does this sign mean?

a   End of motorway
b   End of restriction
c   Lane ends ahead
d   Free recovery ends

Question 11.131

Mark one answer
This sign is advising you to

a   follow the route diversion
b   follow the signs to the picnic area
c   give way to pedestrians
d   give way to cyclists

Question 11.132

Mark one answer
Why would this temporary speed limit sign be shown?

a   To warn of the end of the motorway
b   To warn you of a low bridge
c   To warn you of a junction ahead
d   To warn of road works ahead

Question 11.133

Mark one answer
This traffic sign means there is

a   a compulsory maximum speed limit
b   an advisory maximum speed limit
c   a compulsory minimum speed limit
d   an advised separation distance

Question 11.134

Mark one answer
You see this sign at a crossroads. You should

a   maintain the same speed
b   carry on with great care
c   find another route
d   telephone the police

Question 11.135

Mark one answer
You are signalling to turn right in busy traffic. How would you confirm your intention safely?

a   Sound the horn
b   Give an arm signal
c   Flash your headlights
d   Position over the centre line

Question 11.136

Mark one answer
What does this sign mean?

a   Motorcycles only
b   No cars
c   Cars only
d   No motorcycles

Question 11.137

Mark one answer
You are on a motorway. You see this sign on a lorry that has stopped in the right-hand lane. You should

a   move into the right-hand lane
b   stop behind the flashing lights
c   pass the lorry on the left
d   leave the motorway at the next exit

Question 11.138

Mark one answer
You are on a motorway. Red flashing lights appear above your lane only. What should you do?

a   Continue in that lane and look for further information
b   Move into another lane in good time
c   Pull onto the hard shoulder
d   Stop and wait for an instruction to proceed

Question 11.139

Mark one answer
A red traffic light means

a   you must stop behind the white stop line
b   you may go straight on if there is no other traffic
c   you may turn left if it is safe to do so
d   you must slow down and prepare to stop if traffic has started to cross

Question 11.140

Mark one answer
The driver of this car is giving an arm signal. What are they about to do?

a   Turn to the right
b   Turn to the left
c   Go straight ahead
d   Let pedestrians cross

Question 11.141

Mark one answer
Which arm signal tells you that the car you are following is going to turn left?

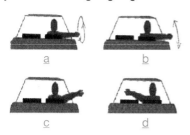

a   b

c   d

Question 11.142

Mark one answer
When may you sound the horn?

a   To give you right of way
b   To attract a friend's attention
c   To warn others of your presence
d   To make slower drivers move over

Question 11.143

Mark one answer
You must not use your horn when you are stationary

a   unless a moving vehicle may cause you danger
b   at any time whatsoever
c   unless it is used only briefly
d   except for signalling that you have just arrived

Question 11.144

Mark one answer
What does this sign mean?

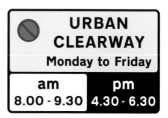

a   You can park on the days and times shown
b   No parking on the days and times shown
c   No parking at all from Monday to Friday
d   End of the urban clearway restrictions

Question 11.145

Mark one answer
What does this sign mean?

a   Quayside or river bank
b   Steep hill downwards
c   Uneven road surface
d   Road liable to flooding

Question 11.146

Mark one answer
You see this amber traffic light ahead. Which light(s) will come on next?

- a Red alone
- b Red and amber together
- c Green and amber together
- d Green alone

Question 11.147

Mark one answer
The white line painted in the centre of the road means

- a oncoming vehicles have priority over you
- b you should give priority to oncoming vehicles
- c there is a hazard ahead of you
- d the area is a national speed limit zone

Question 11.148

Mark one answer
Which sign means you have priority over oncoming vehicles?

a

b

c

d

Question 11.149

Mark one answer
You see this signal overhead on the motorway. What does it mean?

- a Leave the motorway at the next exit
- b All vehicles use the hard shoulder
- c Sharp bend to the left ahead
- d Stop all lanes ahead closed

Question 11.150

Mark one answer

A white line like this along the centre of the road is a

a bus lane marking
b hazard warning
c give way marking
d lane marking

Question 11.151

Mark one answer

What is the purpose of these yellow criss-cross lines on the road?

a To make you more aware of the traffic lights
b To guide you into position as you turn
c To prevent the junction from becoming blocked
d To show you where to stop when the lights change

Question 11.152

Mark one answer

What is the reason for the yellow criss-cross lines painted on the road here?

a To mark out an area for trams only
b To prevent queuing traffic from blocking the junction on the left
c To mark the entrance lane to a car park
d To warn you of the tram lines crossing the road

Question 11.153

Mark one answer
What is the reason for the area marked in red and white along the centre of this road?

a It is to separate traffic flowing in opposite directions
b It marks an area to be used by overtaking motorcyclists
c It is a temporary marking to warn of the roadworks
d It is separating the two sides of the dual carriageway

Question 11.154

Mark one answer
Other drivers may sometimes flash their headlights at you. In which situation are they allowed to do this?

a To warn of a radar speed trap ahead
b To show that they are giving way to you
c To warn you of their presence
d To let you know there is a fault with your vehicle

Question 11.155

Mark three answers
At roadworks which of the following can control traffic flow?

a A STOP–GO board
b Flashing amber lights
c A police officer
d Flashing red lights
e Temporary traffic lights

Answers and explanations

11.1   d
11.2   b
11.3   a
11.4   d
11.5   a
11.6   b
11.7   c
11.8   b
11.9   a
11.10 d
11.11 d
11.12 a Red circles tell you what you must not do. Rectangles usually give you information.
11.13 a
11.14 b
11.15 a
11.16 d
11.17 b
11.18 d
11.19 d
11.20 d
11.21 a
11.22 c
11.23 b
11.24 d
11.25 c
11.26 b
11.27 a There will also be a plate indicating when the restriction applies.
11.28 b
11.29 b
11.30 c
11.31 c This is a clearway sign and you must not stop at all.
11.32 a

11.33 c
11.34 b
11.35 c
11.36 b You must always stop at a stop sign.
11.37 d
11.38 d
11.39 c
11.40 d
11.41 c
11.42 b
11.43 c
11.44 d
11.45 a
11.46 d Circular signs with blue backgrounds tell you what you must do.
11.47 b
11.48 d
11.49 b
11.50 a
11.51 a
11.52 a
11.53 a Red triangles usually give a warning.
11.54 b
11.55 b
11.56 a
11.57 d
11.58 a, c, e, f
11.59 c
11.60 a
11.61 a
11.62 c
11.63 d
11.64 b
11.65 c
11.66 b
11.67 b

11.68 b
11.69 b
11.70 d
11.71 a
11.72 c
11.73 a
11.74 c
11.75 d It is dangerous to overtake when you see this sign because the dip in the road could be hiding oncoming traffic.
11.76 a
11.77 c
11.78 b
11.79 d
11.80 a
11.81 b
11.82 b
11.83 c
11.84 c
11.85 a
11.86 a
11.87 d
11.88 b
11.89 c
11.90 d
11.91 c
11.92 a, c, d
11.93 b
11.94 a The sequence of traffic lights is red, then red and amber, then green, then amber alone, then red.
11.95 c You must always stop at a red traffic light.
11.96 d An amber light means stop, and the lights will next change to red.

11.97 c The next light will be green and you must wait until it appears before moving.
11.98 b
11.99 a
11.100 a
11.101 c
11.102 b, d, f
11.103 a
11.104 c
11.105 c
11.106 b
11.107 b
11.108 a Long lines with short gaps between them in the middle of the road are hazard warning lines. The more paint the more danger.
11.109 c Because the major road is on a bend, your vision is restricted to both left and right.

11.110 a
11.111 b
11.112 a
11.113 b You must stop, but 'c' is wrong because it may not be safe to stop immediately.
11.114 d
11.115 d
11.116 b
11.117 a You must not overtake on the left on a motorway or dual carriageway unless you are moving in queues of slow-moving traffic.
11.118 a Obviously you must make sure it is safe before doing so.
11.119 d

11.120 c Always look well ahead and
you will have plenty of time to
react.

11.121 d

11.122 c

11.123 b

11.124 c

11.125 c

11.126 a

11.127 b

11.128 d

11.129 b

11.130 b

11.131 a

11.132 d

11.133 a

11.134 b

11.135 b

11.136 d

11.137 c

11.138 b You must go no further in that
lane. You may change lanes
and proceed, unless flashing
red lights appear above all of
them.

11.139 a

11.140 b

11.141 a

11.142 c

11.143 a

11.144 b

11.145 a

11.146 a

11.147 c

11.148 c

11.149 a

11.150 b

11.151 c

11.152 b

11.153 a

11.154 c

11.155 a, c, e

Theory Test Questions for Motorcyclists

2003–2004

Section 12   Documents

Question 12.1 NI Exempt

Mark one answer

After passing your motorcycle test you must exchange the pass certificate for a full motorcycle licence within

a six months
b one year
c two years
d five years

Question 12.2

Mark two answers

For which TWO of these must you show your motorcycle insurance certificate?

a When you are taking your motorcycle test
b When buying or selling a machine
c When a police officer asks you for it
d When you are taxing your machine
e When having an MOT inspection

Question 12.3

Mark one answer

When you buy a motorcycle you will need a vehicle registration document from

a any MOT testing station
b the person selling the motorcycle
c your local council offices
d your local trading standards officer

Question 12.4

Mark one answer

You are a learner motorcyclist. The law states that you can carry a passenger when

a your motorcycle is no larger than 125cc
b your pillion passenger is a full licence-holder
c you have passed your test for a full licence
d you have had three years' experience of riding

Question 12.5

Mark three answers

You hold a provisional motorcycle licence. This means you must NOT

a exceed 30mph
b ride on a motorway
c ride after dark
d carry a pillion passenger
e ride without 'L' plates displayed

Question 12.6

Mark three answers

Which of the following information is found on your motorcycle registration document?

a   Make and model
b   Service history record
c   Ignition key security number
d   Engine size and number
e   Purchase price
f   Year of first registration

Question 12.7

Mark one answer

A theory test pass certificate is valid for

a   two years
b   three years
c   four years
d   five years

Question 12.8 NI Exempt

Mark one answer

Compulsory Basic Training (CBT) can only be carried out by

a   any ADI (Approved Driving Instructor)
b   any road safety officer
c   any DSA (Driving Standards Agency) approved training body
d   any motorcycle main dealer

Question 12.9

Mark one answer

A full category A1 licence will allow you to ride a motorcycle up to

a   125cc
b   250cc
c   350cc
d   425cc

Question 12.10

Mark one answer

Before riding anyone else's motorcycle you should make sure that

a   the owner has third party insurance cover
b   your own motorcycle has insurance cover
c   the motorcycle is insured for your use
d   the owner has the insurance documents with them

Question 12.11

Mark one answer

Vehicle excise duty is often called 'Road Tax' or 'The Tax Disc'. You must

a   keep it with your registration document
b   display it clearly on your motorcycle
c   keep it concealed safely in your motorcycle
d   carry it on you at all times

Question 12.12 NI Exempt

Mark one answer
Motorcycles must FIRST have an MOT test certificate when they are

a one year old
b three years old
c five years old
d seven years old

Question 12.13

Mark one answer
Your motorcycle needs a current MOT certificate. You do not have one. Until you do have one you will not be able to renew your

a driving licence
b motorcycle insurance
c road tax disc
d motorcycle registration document

Question 12.14

Mark three answers
Which THREE of the following do you need before you can ride legally?

a A valid driving licence with signature
b A valid tax disc displayed on your motorcycle
c Proof of your identity
d Proper insurance cover
e Breakdown cover
f A vehicle handbook

Question 12.15

Mark three answers
Which THREE pieces of information are found on a registration document?

a Registered keeper
b Make of the motorcycle
c Service history details
d Date of the MOT
e Type of insurance cover
f Engine size

Question 12.16

Mark three answers
You have a duty to contact the licensing authority when

a you go abroad on holiday
b you change your motorcycle
c you change your name
d your job status is changed
e your permanent address changes
f your job involves travelling abroad

Question 12.17

Mark two answers
Your motorcycle is insured third party only. This covers

a damage to your motorcycle
b damage to other vehicles
c injury to yourself
d injury to others
e all damage and injury

194

Question 12.18

You have just bought a secondhand motorcycle. When should you tell the licensing authority of change of ownership?

a   Immediately
b   After 28 days
c   When an MOT is due
d   Only when you insure it

Question 12.19

Your motorcycle insurance policy has an excess of £100. What does this mean?

a   The insurance company will pay the first £100 of any claim
b   You will be paid £100 if you do not have an accident
c   Your motorcycle is insured for a value of £100 if it is stolen
d   You will have to pay the first £100 of any claim

Question 12.20

When you apply to renew your motorcycle excise licence (tax disc) you must produce

a   a valid insurance certificate
b   the old tax disc
c   the motorcycle handbook
d   a valid driving licence

Question 12.21

What is the legal minimum insurance cover you must have to ride on public roads?

a   Third party, fire and theft
b   Fully comprehensive
c   Third party only
d   Personal injury cover

Question 12.22 NI Exempt

You have a CBT (Compulsory Basic Training) certificate issued from 1st February 2001. How long will this be valid for?

a   1 year
b   2 years
c   3 years
d   4 years

Question 12.23

Mark one answer

Your motorcycle road tax is due to expire. As well as the renewal form and fee you will also need to produce an MOT (if required). What else will you need?

a   Proof of purchase receipt
b   Compulsory Basic Training certificate
c   A valid certificate of insurance
d   The Vehicle Registration Document

Question 12.24

Mark one answer

You buy a second-hand motorcycle. What document should be supplied with it?

a   A Compulsory Basic Training certificate
b   A personal injury cover note
c   A Vehicle Registration Document
d   A full service history pack

Question 12.25

Mark one answer

A Vehicle Registration Document will show

a   the service history
b   the year of first registration
c   the purchase price
d   the tyre sizes

Question 12.26

Mark one answer

Which one of these details would you expect to see on an MOT?

a   Your name, address and telephone number
b   The vehicle registration and chassis number
c   The previous owner's details
d   The next due date for servicing

Question 12.27

Mark one answer

What is the purpose of having a vehicle test certificate (MOT)?

a   To make sure your motorcycle is roadworthy
b   To certify how many miles per gallon it does
c   To prove you own the motorcycle
d   To allow you to park in restricted areas

Question 12.28 NI Exempt

Mark one answer
You want a licence to ride a large motorcycle via Direct Access. You will

a   not require L plates if you have passed a car test
b   require L plates only when learning on your own machine
c   require L plates while learning with a qualified instructor
d   not require L plates if you have passed a moped test

Question 12.29

Mark one answer
A theory test pass certificate will not be valid after

a   6 months
b   1 year
c   18 months
d   2 years

Question 12.30 NI Exempt

Mark one answer
Before taking a practical motorcycle test you need

a   a full moped licence
b   a full car licence
c   a CBT (Compulsory Basic Training) certificate
d   12 months' riding experience

Question 12.31

Mark three answers
You must notify the licensing authority when

a   your health affects your riding
b   your eyesight does not meet a set standard
c   you intend lending your motorcycle
d   your motorcycle requires an MOT certificate
e   you change your motorcycle

Question 12.32

Mark two answers
You have just passed your practical motorcycle test. This is your first full licence. Within two years you get six penalty points. You will have to

a   retake only your theory test
b   retake your theory and practical tests
c   retake only your practical test
d   reapply for your full licence immediately
e   reapply for your provisional licence

Question 12.33 NI Exempt

Mark three answers
A motorcyclist may only carry a pillion passenger when

a the rider has successfully completed CBT (Compulsory Basic Training)
b the rider holds a full licence for the category of motorcycle
c the motorcycle is fitted with rear foot pegs
d the rider has a full car licence and is over 21
e there is a proper passenger seat fitted
f there is no sidecar fitted to the machine

Question 12.34

Mark one answer
An MOT certificate is normally valid for

a three years after the date it was issued
b 10,000 miles
c one year after the date it was issued
d 30,000 miles

Question 12.35

Mark one answer
A cover note is a document issued before you receive your

a driving licence
b insurance certificate
c registration document
d MOT certificate

Question 12.36 NI Exempt

Mark one answer
A police officer asks to see your documents. You do not have them with you. You may produce them at a police station within

a five days
b seven days
c 14 days
d 21 days

Question 12.37

Mark two answers
You have just passed your practical test. You do not hold a full licence in another category. Within two years you get six penalty points on your licence. What will you have to do?

a Retake only your theory test
b Retake your theory and practical tests
c Retake only your practical test
d Reapply for your full licence immediately
e Reapply for your provisional licence

12.1   c
12.2   c, d
12.3   b
12.4   c
12.5   b, d, e
12.6   a, d, f
12.7   a
12.8   c
12.9   a
12.10 c Your own motorbike insurance is very unlikely to cover you to drive another person's motorbike.
12.11 b
12.12 b
12.13 c
12.14 a, b, d
12.15 a, b, f
12.16 b, c, e
12.17 b, d
12.18 a
12.19 d
12.20 a
12.21 c
12.22 b
12.23 c
12.24 c
12.25 b
12.26 b
12.27 a
12.28 c
12.29 d
12.30 c
12.31 a, b, e
12.32 b, e
12.33 b, c, e
12.34 c

199

12.35 b

12.36 b You may select the police
         station of your choice.

12.37 b, e

Theory Test Questions for Motorcyclists

2003–2004

Section 13   Accidents

Question 13.1

Mark one answer
Your motorcycle has broken down on a motorway. How will you know the direction of the nearest emergency telephone?

a   By walking with the flow of traffic
b   By following an arrow on a marker post
c   By walking against the flow of traffic
d   By remembering where the last phone was

Question 13.2

Mark one answer
You are travelling on a motorway. A bag falls from your motorcycle. There are valuables in the bag. What should you do?

a   Go back carefully and collect the bag as quickly as possible
b   Stop wherever you are and pick up the bag, but only when there is a safe gap
c   Stop on the hard shoulder and use the emergency telephone to inform the police
d   Stop on the hard shoulder and then retrieve the bag yourself

Question 13.3

Mark one answer
You should use the engine cut-out switch to

a   stop the engine in an emergency
b   stop the engine on short journeys
c   save wear on the ignition switch
d   start the engine if you lose the key

Question 13.4

Mark one answer
You are involved in an accident. How can you reduce the risk of fire to your motorcycle?

a   Keep the engine running
b   Open the choke
c   Turn the fuel tap to reserve
d   Use the engine cut out switch

Question 13.5

Mark one answer
You are riding on a motorway. The car in front switches on its hazard warning lights whilst moving. This means

a   they are going to take the next exit
b   there is a danger ahead
c   there is a police car in the left lane
d   they are trying to change lanes

Question 13.6

Mark one answer

You are on the motorway. Luggage falls from your motorcycle. What should you do?

a   Stop at the next emergency telephone and contact the police
b   Stop on the motorway and put on hazard lights whilst you pick it up
c   Walk back up the motorway to pick it up
d   Pull up on the hard shoulder and wave traffic down

Question 13.7

Mark four answers

You are involved in an accident with another vehicle. Someone is injured. Your motorcycle is damaged. Which FOUR of the following should you find out?

a   Whether the driver owns the other vehicle involved
b   The other driver's name, address and telephone number
c   The make and registration number of the other vehicle
d   The occupation of the other driver
e   The details of the other driver's vehicle insurance
f   Whether the other driver is licensed to drive

Question 13.8

Mark three answers

You have broken down on a motorway. When you use the emergency telephone you will be asked

a   for the number on the telephone that you are using
b   for your driving licence details
c   for the name of your vehicle insurance company
d   for details of yourself and your motorcycle
e   whether you belong to a motoring organisation

Question 13.9

Mark one answer

You are on a motorway. When can you use hazard warning lights?

a   When a vehicle is following too closely
b   When you slow down quickly because of danger ahead
c   When you are being towed by another vehicle
d   When riding on the hard shoulder

Question 13.10

Mark one answer

Your motorcycle breaks down in a tunnel. What should you do?

a Stay with your motorcycle and wait for the police
b Stand in the lane behind your motorcycle to warn others
c Stand in front of your motorcycle to warn oncoming drivers
d Switch on hazard lights then go and call for help immediately

Question 13.11

Mark one answer

You are riding through a tunnel. Your motorcycle breaks down. What should you do?

a Switch on hazard warning lights
b Remain on your motorcycle
c Wait for the police to find you
d Rely on CCTV cameras seeing you

Question 13.12

Mark one answer

At the scene of an accident you should

a not put yourself at risk
b go to those casualties who are screaming
c pull everybody out of their vehicles
d leave vehicle engines switched on

Question 13.13

Mark four answers

You are the first to arrive at the scene of an accident. Which FOUR of these should you do?

a Leave as soon as another motorist arrives
b Switch off the vehicle engine(s)
c Move uninjured people away from the vehicle(s)
d Call the emergency services
e Warn other traffic

Question 13.14

Mark one answer

An accident has just happened. An injured person is lying in the busy road. What is the FIRST thing you should do to help?

a Treat the person for shock
b Warn other traffic
c Place them in the recovery position
d Make sure the injured person is kept warm

Question 13.15

Mark three answers
You are the first person to arrive at an accident where people are badly injured. Which THREE should you do?

a Switch on your own hazard warning lights
b Make sure that someone telephones for an ambulance
c Try and get people who are injured to drink something
d Move the people who are injured clear of their vehicles
e Get people who are not injured clear of the scene

Question 13.16

Mark one answer
You arrive at the scene of a motorcycle accident. The rider is injured. When should the helmet be removed?

a Only when it is essential
b Always straight away
c Only when the motorcyclist asks
d Always, unless they are in shock

Question 13.17

Mark three answers
You arrive at a serious motorcycle accident. The motorcyclist is unconscious and bleeding. Your main priorities should be to

a try to stop the bleeding
b make a list of witnesses
c check the casualty's breathing
d take the numbers of the vehicles involved
e sweep up any loose debris
f check the casualty's airways

Question 13.18

Mark one answer
You arrive at an accident. A motorcyclist is unconscious. Your FIRST priority is the casualty's

a breathing
b bleeding
c broken bones
d bruising

Question 13.19

Mark three answers

At an accident a casualty is unconscious. Which THREE of the following should you check urgently?

a Circulation
b Airway
c Shock
d Breathing
e Broken bones

Question 13.20

Mark three answers

You arrive at the scene of an accident. It has just happened and someone is unconscious. Which of the following should be given urgent priority to help them?

a Clear the airway and keep it open
b Try to get them to drink water
c Check that they are breathing
d Look for any witnesses
e Stop any heavy bleeding
f Take the numbers of vehicles involved

Question 13.21

Mark three answers

At an accident someone is unconscious. Your main priorities should be to

a sweep up the broken glass
b take the names of witnesses
c count the number of vehicles involved
d check the airway is clear
e make sure they are breathing
f stop any heavy bleeding

Question 13.22

Mark three answers

You have stopped at the scene of an accident to give help. Which THREE things should you do?

a Keep injured people warm and comfortable
b Keep injured people calm by talking to them reassuringly
c Keep injured people on the move by walking them around
d Give injured people a warm drink
e Make sure that injured people are not left alone

Question 13.23

Mark three answers
You arrive at the scene of an accident. It has just happened and someone is injured. Which THREE of the following should be given urgent priority?

a   Stop any severe bleeding
b   Get them a warm drink
c   Check that their breathing is OK
d   Take numbers of vehicles involved
e   Look for witnesses
f   Clear their airway and keep it open

Question 13.24

Mark two answers
At an accident a casualty has stopped breathing. You should

a   remove anything that is blocking the mouth
b   keep the head tilted forwards as far as possible
c   raise the legs to help with circulation
d   try to give the casualty something to drink
e   keep the head tilted back as far as possible

Question 13.25

Mark four answers
You are at the scene of an accident. Someone is suffering from shock. You should

a   reassure them constantly
b   offer them a cigarette
c   keep them warm
d   avoid moving them if possible
e   loosen any tight clothing
f   give them a warm drink

Question 13.26

Mark one answer
Which of the following should you NOT do at the scene of an accident?

a   Warn other traffic by switching on your hazard warning lights
b   Call the emergency services immediately
c   Offer someone a cigarette to calm them down
d   Ask drivers to switch off their engines

Question 13.27

Mark two answers

There has been an accident. The driver is suffering from shock. You should

a give them a drink
b reassure them
c not leave them alone
d offer them a cigarette
e ask who caused the accident

Question 13.28

Mark three answers

You are at the scene of an accident. Someone is suffering from shock. You should

a offer them a cigarette
b offer them a warm drink
c keep them warm
d loosen any tight clothing
e reassure them constantly

Question 13.29

Mark one answer

You have to treat someone for shock at the scene of an accident. You should

a reassure them constantly
b walk them around to calm them down
c give them something cold to drink
d cool them down as soon as possible

Question 13.30

Mark one answer

You arrive at the scene of a motorcycle accident. No other vehicle is involved. The rider is unconscious, lying in the middle of the road. The first thing you should do is

a move the rider out of the road
b warn other traffic
c clear the road of debris
d give the rider reassurance

Question 13.31

Mark one answer

At an accident a small child is not breathing. When giving mouth to mouth you should breathe

a sharply
b gently
c heavily
d rapidly

Question 13.32

Mark three answers

To start mouth to mouth on a casualty you should

a tilt their head forward
b clear the airway
c turn them on their side
d tilt their head back
e pinch the nostrils together
f put their arms across their chest

Question 13.33

Mark one answer

When you are giving mouth to mouth you should only stop when

a you think the casualty is dead
b the casualty can breathe without help
c the casualty has turned blue
d you think the ambulance is coming

Question 13.34

Mark one answer

You arrive at the scene of an accident. There has been an engine fire and someone's hands and arms have been burnt. You should NOT

a douse the burn thoroughly with cool liquid
b lay the casualty down
c remove anything sticking to the burn
d reassure them constantly

Question 13.35

Mark one answer

You arrive at an accident where someone is suffering from severe burns. You should

a apply lotions to the injury
b burst any blisters
c remove anything stuck to the burns
d douse the burns with cool liquid

Question 13.36

Mark two answers

You arrive at the scene of an accident. A pedestrian has a severe bleeding wound on their leg, although it is not broken. What should you do?

a Dab the wound to stop bleeding
b Keep both legs flat on the ground
c Apply firm pressure to the wound
d Raise the leg to lessen bleeding
e Fetch them a warm drink

Question 13.37

You arrive at the scene of an accident. A passenger is bleeding badly from an arm wound. What should you do?

a Apply pressure over the wound and keep the arm down
b Dab the wound
c Get them a drink
d Apply pressure over the wound and raise the arm

Question 13.38

You arrive at the scene of an accident. A pedestrian is bleeding heavily from a leg wound but the leg is not broken. What should you do?

a Dab the wound to stop the bleeding
b Keep both legs flat on the ground
c Apply firm pressure to the wound
d Fetch them a warm drink

Question 13.39

At an accident a casualty is unconscious but still breathing. You should only move them if

a an ambulance is on its way
b bystanders advise you to
c there is further danger
d bystanders will help you to

Question 13.40

At an accident you suspect a casualty has back injuries. The area is safe. You should

a offer them a drink
b not move them
c raise their legs
d offer them a cigarette

Question 13.41

At an accident it is important to look after the casualty. When the area is safe, you should

a get them out of the vehicle
b give them a drink
c give them something to eat
d keep them in the vehicle

Question 13.42

Mark one answer

A tanker is involved in an accident. Which sign would show that the tanker is carrying dangerous goods?

a

b

c

d

Question 13.43

Mark three answers

The police may ask you to produce which three of these documents following an accident?

a Vehicle registration document
b Driving licence
c Theory test certificate
d Insurance certificate
e MOT test certificate
f Road tax disc

Question 13.44

Mark one answer

At a railway level crossing the red light signal continues to flash after a train has gone by. What should you do?

a Phone the signal operator
b Alert drivers behind you
c Wait
d Proceed with caution

Question 13.45

Mark one answer

You see a car on the hard shoulder of a motorway with a HELP pennant displayed. This means the driver is most likely to be

a a disabled person
b first aid trained
c a foreign visitor
d a rescue patrol person

Question 13.46

Mark one answer

On the motorway the hard shoulder should be used

a to answer a mobile phone
b when an emergency arises
c for a short rest when tired
d to check a road atlas

211

Question 13.47

Mark two answers

For which TWO should you use hazard warning lights?

a   When you slow down quickly on a motorway because of a hazard ahead
b   When you have broken down
c   When you wish to stop on double yellow lines
d   When you need to park on the pavement

Question 13.48

Mark one answer

When are you allowed to use hazard warning lights?

a   When stopped and temporarily obstructing traffic
b   When travelling during darkness without headlights
c   When parked for shopping on double yellow lines
d   When travelling slowly because you are lost

Question 13.49

Mark one answer

You are on a motorway. A large box falls onto the road from a lorry. The lorry does not stop. You should

a   go to the next emergency telephone and inform the police
b   catch up with the lorry and try to get the driver's attention
c   stop close to the box until the police arrive
d   pull over to the hard shoulder, then remove the box

Question 13.50

Mark one answer

There has been an accident. A motorcyclist is lying injured and unconscious. Why should you usually not attempt to remove their helmet?

a   Because they may not want you to
b   This could result in more serious injury
c   They will get too cold if you do this
d   Because you could scratch the helmet

Question 13.51

Mark one answer

After an accident, someone is unconscious in their vehicle. When should you call the emergency services?

a Only as a last resort
b As soon as possible
c After you have woken them up
d After checking for broken bones

Question 13.52

Mark one answer

An accident casualty has an injured arm. They can move it freely, but it is bleeding. Why should you get them to keep it in a raised position?

a Because it will ease the pain
b It will help them to be seen more easily
c To stop them touching other people
d It will help to reduce the bleeding

Question 13.53

Mark one answer

You are going through a congested tunnel and have to stop. What should you do?

a Pull up very close to the vehicle in front to save space
b Ignore any message signs as they are never up to date
c Keep a safe distance from the vehicle in front
d Make a U-turn and find another route

Question 13.54

Mark one answer

You are going through a tunnel. What should you look out for that warns of accidents or congestion?

a Hazard warning lines
b Other drivers flashing their lights
c Variable message signs
d Areas marked with hatch markings

Question 13.55

Mark one answer

You are going through a tunnel. What systems are provided to warn of any accidents or congestion?

a Double white centre lines
b Variable message signs
c Chevron 'distance markers'
d Rumble strips

13.1	b
13.2	c It would be extremely dangerous to try and retrieve the bag yourself.
13.3	a The engine cut-out switch stops the engine and shuts off all electrical circuits, thus reducing the risk of fire in an accident.
13.4	d
13.5	b
13.6	a
13.7	a, b, c, e
13.8	a, d, e
13.9	b
13.10	d
13.11	a
13.12	a
13.13	b, c, d, e
13.14	b Warning other traffic first helps stop the accident getting even worse.
13.15	a, b, e
13.16	a
13.17	a, c, f
13.18	a
13.19	a, b, d
13.20	a, c, e Note that these are the things to which you should give urgent priority.
13.21	d, e, f
13.22	a, b, e You should not move injured people unless they are in danger; nor should you give them anything to drink.
13.23	a, c, f
13.24	a, e

13.25	a, c, d, e
13.26	c
13.27	b, c
13.28	c, d, e
13.29	a
13.30	b Note that this is the FIRST thing to do. By warning other traffic you help reduce the risk of more collisions.
13.31	b
13.32	b, d, e
13.33	b
13.34	c
13.35	d
13.36	c, d
13.37	d
13.38	c
13.39	c
13.40	b If you move the casualty you may worsen their injury.
13.41	d
13.42	b
13.43	b, d, e
13.44	c This usually means another train is coming.
13.45	a
13.46	b
13.47	a, b
13.48	a
13.49	a
13.50	b
13.51	b
13.52	d
13.53	c
13.54	c
13.55	b

Theory Test Questions for Motorcyclists

2003–2004

Motorcycle loading

Question 14.1

Mark one answer
If a trailer swerves or snakes when you are towing it you should

a   ease off the throttle and reduce your speed
b   let go of the handlebars and let it correct itself
c   brake hard and hold the brake on
d   increase your speed as quickly as possible

Question 14.2

Mark two answers
When riding with a sidecar attached for the first time you should

a   keep your speed down
b   be able to stop more quickly
c   accelerate quickly round bends
d   approach corners more carefully

Question 14.3

Mark one answer
When may a learner motorcyclist carry a pillion passenger?

a   If the passenger holds a full licence
b   Not at any time
c   If the rider is undergoing training
d   If the passenger is over 21

Question 14.4

Mark three answers
Which THREE must a learner motorcyclist under 21 NOT do?

a   Ride a motorcycle with an engine capacity greater than 125cc
b   Pull a trailer
c   Carry a pillion passenger
d   Ride faster than 30mph
e   Use the right-hand lane on dual carriageways

Question 14.5

Mark three answers
When carrying extra weight on a motorcycle, you may need to make adjustments to the

a   headlight
b   gears
c   suspension
d   tyres
e   footrests

Question 14.6 NI Exempt

Mark one answer
To obtain the full category 'A' licence through the accelerated or direct access scheme, your motorcycle must be

a solo with maximum power 25kw (33 bhp)
b solo with maximum power of 11kw (14.6 bhp)
c fitted with a sidecar and have minimum power of 35kw (46.6 bhp)
d solo with minimum power of 35 kw (46.6 bhp)

Question 14.7

Mark one answer
Any load that is carried on a luggage rack MUST be

a securely fastened when riding
b carried only when strictly necessary
c visible when you are riding
d covered with plastic sheeting

Question 14.8

Mark one answer
Pillion passengers should

a have a provisional motorcycle licence
b be lighter than the rider
c always wear a helmet
d signal for the rider

Question 14.9

Mark one answer
Pillion passengers should

a give the rider directions
b lean with the rider when going round bends
c check the road behind for the rider
d give arm signals for the rider

Question 14.10

Mark one answer
When you are going around a corner your pillion passenger should

a give arm signals for you
b check behind for other vehicles
c lean with you on bends
d lean to one side to see ahead

Question 14.11

Mark one answer
Which of these may need to be adjusted when carrying a pillion passenger?

a Indicators
b Exhaust
c Fairing
d Headlight

Question 14.12

Mark one answer

You are towing a trailer with your motorcycle. You should remember that your

a   stopping distance may increase
b   fuel consumption will improve
c   tyre grip will increase
d   stability will improve

Question 14.13

Mark one answer

Carrying a heavy load in your top box may

a   cause high speed weave
b   cause a puncture
c   use less fuel
d   improve stability

Question 14.14

Mark one answer

Heavy loads in a motorcycle top box may

a   improve stability
b   cause low-speed wobble
c   cause a puncture
d   improve braking

Question 14.15

Mark two answers

You want to tow a trailer behind your motorcycle. You should

a   display a 'long vehicle' sign
b   fit a larger battery
c   have a full motorcycle licence
d   ensure that your engine is more than 125cc
e   ensure that your motorcycle has shaft drive

Question 14.16

Mark two answers
Overloading your motorcycle can seriously affect the

a   gearbox
b   steering
c   handling
d   battery life
e   journey time

Question 14.17

Mark one answer
Who is responsible for making sure that a motorcycle is not overloaded?

a   The rider of the motorcycle
b   The owner of the items being carried
c   The licensing authority
d   The owner of the motorcycle

Question 14.18

Mark one answer
Before fitting a sidecar to a motorcycle you should

a   have the wheels balanced
b   have the engine tuned
c   pass the extended bike test
d   check that the motorcycle is suitable

Question 14.19

Mark one answer
You are using throwover saddlebags. Why is it important to make sure they are evenly loaded?

a   They will be uncomfortable for you to sit on
b   They will slow your motorcycle down
c   They could make your motorcycle unstable
d   They will be uncomfortable for a pillion passenger to sit on

Question 14.20

Mark one answer
You are carrying a bulky tank bag. What could this affect?

a   Your ability to steer
b   Your ability to accelerate
c   Your view ahead
d   Your insurance premium

Question 14.21

Mark one answer
To carry a pillion passenger you must

a   hold a full car licence
b   hold a full motorcycle licence
c   be over the age of 21
d   be over the age of 25

Question 14.22

Mark one answer

When carrying a heavy load on your luggage rack, you may need to adjust your

a carburettor
b fuel tap
c seating position
d tyre pressures

Question 14.23

Mark one answer

You are carrying a pillion passenger. When following other traffic, which of the following should you do?

a Keep to your normal following distance
b Get your passenger to keep checking behind
c Keep further back than you normally would
d Get your passenger to signal for you

Question 14.24

Mark one answer

You should only carry a child as a pillion passenger when

a they are over 14 years old
b they are over 16 years old
c they can reach the floor from the seat
d they can reach the handholds and footrests

Question 14.25

Mark one answer

You have fitted a sidecar to your motorcycle. You should make sure that the sidecar

a has a registration plate
b is correctly aligned
c has a waterproof cover
d has a solid cover

Question 14.26

Mark one answer

You are riding a motorcycle and sidecar. The extra weight

a will allow you to corner more quickly
b will allow you to brake later for hazards
c may increase your stopping distance
d will improve your fuel consumption

Question 14.27

Mark one answer

You are carrying a pillion passenger. To allow for the extra weight, which of the following is most likely to need adjustment?

a Preload on the front forks
b Preload on the rear shock absorber(s)
c The balance of the rear wheel
d The front and rear wheel alignment

Question 14.28

Mark one answer

A trailer on a motorcycle must be no wider than

a   0.5 metres (1 foot 8 inches)
b   1 metre (3 feet 3 inches)
c   1.5 metres (4 feet 11 inches)
d   2 metres (6 feet 6 inches)

Question 14.29

Mark two answers

To carry a pillion passenger your motorcycle should be fitted with

a   rear footrests
b   an engine of 250cc or over
c   a top box
d   a grab handle
e   a proper pillion seat

Question 14.30

Mark one answer

You want to tow a trailer with your motorcycle. Which one applies?

a   The motorcycle should be attached to a sidecar
b   The trailer should weigh more than the motorcycle
c   The trailer should be fitted with brakes
d   The trailer should NOT be more than 1 metre (3 feet 3 inches) wide

Question 14.31

Mark three answers

Your motorcycle is fitted with a top box. It is unwise to carry a heavy load in the top box because it may

a   reduce stability
b   improve stability
c   make turning easier
d   cause high-speed weave
e   cause low-speed wobble
f   increase fuel economy

Question 14.32

Mark one answer

You have a sidecar fitted to your motorcycle. What effect will it have?

a   Reduce stability
b   Make steering lighter
c   Increase stopping distance
d   Increase fuel economy

Question 14.33

Mark two answers

You are towing a small trailer on a busy three-lane motorway. All the lanes are open. You must

a   not exceed 60mph
b   not overtake
c   have a stabiliser fitted
d   use only the left and centre lanes

Answers and explanations

14.1   a

14.2   a, d You will need to adapt your riding technique when riding a bike with a side-car, particularly on bends and when turning. The side-car must be steered because you cannot lean the machine over.

14.3   b

14.4   a, b, c

14.5   a, c, d

14.6   d

14.7   a

14.8   c

14.9   b

14.10   c

14.11   d

14.12   a

14.13   a

14.14   b

14.15   c, d

14.16   b, c

14.17   a

14.18   d

14.19   c

14.20   a

14.21   b

14.22   d

14.23   c

14.24   d

14.25   b

14.26   c

14.27   b

14.28   b

14.29   a, e

14.30   d Also, the laden weight of the trailer must not exceed 150kg or two-thirds of the kerbside weight of the motorcycle, whichever is less.

14.31   a, d, e

14.32   c The side-car is extra weight and is likely to increase your overall stopping distance.

14.33   a, d

Section 15   Useful information

- The routes to a motorcycle licence
- What is CBT?
- What is DAS?
- How do I know where to go for my training?
- What about clothing?
- How do I choose a bike?

The routes to a motorcycle licence

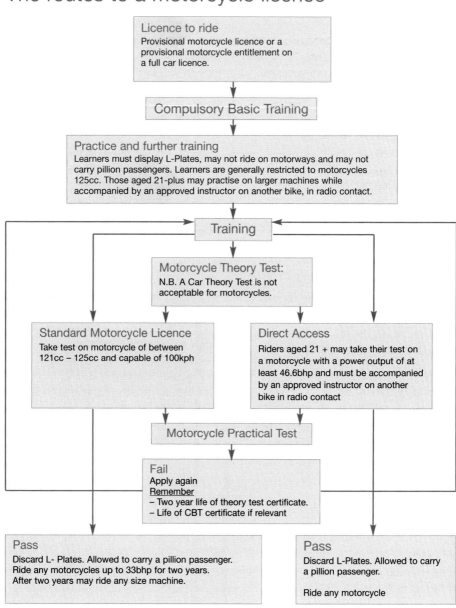

Licence to ride
Provisional motorcycle licence or a provisional motorcycle entitlement on a full car licence.

Compulsory Basic Training

Practice and further training
Learners must display L-Plates, may not ride on motorways and may not carry pillion passengers. Learners are generally restricted to motorcycles 125cc. Those aged 21-plus may practise on larger machines while accompanied by an approved instructor on another bike, in radio contact.

Training

Motorcycle Theory Test:
N.B. A Car Theory Test is not acceptable for motorcycles.

Standard Motorcycle Licence
Take test on motorcycle of between 121cc – 125cc and capable of 100kph

Direct Access
Riders aged 21 + may take their test on a motorcycle with a power output of at least 46.6bhp and must be accompanied by an approved instructor on another bike in radio contact

Motorcycle Practical Test

Fail
Apply again
<u>Remember</u>
– Two year life of theory test certificate.
– Life of CBT certificate if relevant

Pass
Discard L- Plates. Allowed to carry a pillion passenger.
Ride any motorcycles up to 33bhp for two years.
After two years may ride any size machine.

Pass
Discard L-Plates. Allowed to carry a pillion passenger.

Ride any motorcycle

What is Compulsory Basic Training (CBT)?

CBT was introduced in December 1990 to improve motorcycle safety. To this end the course has been highly successful. Ever since February 2001, anybody wanting to ride a two-wheel vehicle is required to undertake the course prior to riding on the road*. The course is set out into 5 modules:

Module 1: The initial part of the day is spent going through the legalities for riding a two-wheeler and you also get the opportunity to learn about the different types of protective clothing available for today's rider.

Module 2: This introduces you to your machine and you learn where everything is on a motorcycle and what it all does.

Module 3: Here you have the opportunity to ride and stop the machine and also begin to go through some basic manoeuvres using the slow riding techniques that we will teach you. You are also taught how to do a U-turn, emergency stop and you practise left and right turns.

Module 4: Pre-road briefing.

Module 5: Put all of your new-found skills into practice with a minimum of two hours on the road with your instructor using the latest radios to stay in touch.

On successful completion of the course you are issued with a DL196 (CBT certificate) that enables you to ride legally on the road on your provisional motorcycle licence. The Certificate lasts for two years from the date of issue and it must be repeated on its expiry unless a Motorcycle Practical Test has been passed in the meantime**.

The CBT is what it says it is and BSM advise that even if you are not intending to continue to gain a full licence that you consider further training like the BSM CBT + course which can cover school or commuter runs, extended road practice Hazard Awareness, safe filtering and much more.

It is often considered that CBT is all you need and it is comprehensive, but further training can only increase your confidence, safety and therefore enjoyment.

A person of 16 years or over can complete a CBT and then ride a scooter or motorcycle on a provisional licence. The size of bike does depend on the age of the person.

* The only exceptions are full car licence holders who wish to ride a moped and passed their car test prior to 1st February 2001.

** Every effort will be made to complete the course in one day but there is no guarantee of this. The instructor has to be assured of competence and safety before issuing the DL 196. It is illegal to offer guarantees of this nature.

What is DAS?

DAS is short for Direct Access and is a route to a full motorcycle licence for people 21 years or over.

Effectively, DAS is a faster way to a full licence (hence the age restriction). CBT and the Theory Test still have to be completed and passed but the Practical Test is then taken on a motorcycle, typically a 500cc machine capable of a power output of at least 35kw.

To pass a DAS Test you have to prove to the examiner that you have developed the necessary skills to handle a larger machine and its power without having to spend time on a smaller motorcycle. Once you have passed a DAS Test you are entitled to ride any size of motorcycle or scooter, so the quality of the training is absolutely essential to your success and safety. Like CBT, you cannot receive training or accompanied practice on a large motorcycle other than by a qualified DAS instructor.

When training, the instructor is restricted to taking no more than two trainees at any one time, and the trainees must be in radio communication with the instructor and be able to clearly hear all directions and prompts.

– The instructor is restricted to taking no more than two trainees at a time.

The only other way to gain a full motorcycle licence is to take a test on a smaller machine, between 121cc and 125cc, and after passing, you are restricted to a machine with a power output of no more than 25kw for two years. After this time your licence automatically converts to a full licence as if you had taken a DAS course. The Restricted Test – as it is sometimes known – can be taken from the age of 17 years and is therefore attractive to younger people, who need that all-important experience before riding a large-power machine.

How do I know where to go for my training?

– Always check instructors' DSA certificates to ensure they are qualified.

Motorcycle training is more heavily regulated than driver training and in most circumstances it would be illegal to learn or even practise with friends or family.

For an organisation such as BSM to become a Motorcycle Training School it has to achieve an Approved Training Body Status, and this is decided by the Driving Standards Agency (DSA).

To become an approved organisation you have to prove that there are suitable off-road sites available to conduct the CBT, and properly qualified instructors to deliver the training. Only organisations that are approved can deliver CBT and DAS training and issue CBT certificates.

Motorcycle instructors allowed to deliver

CBT either hold a yellow card with just a serial number or a yellow card with the serial number followed by the letter C. Either is qualified to train new riders. The Instructor with the C on the Card will have passed a two-day assessment from the DSA and is also entitled to train other instructors.

To give training for DAS, the instructor will have successfully completed a further assessment with the DSA and possess a blue certificate with the serial number starting with D and ending in C. You can ask to see these certificates to confirm that authorised instructors are teaching you.

229

Just like any business, public liability insurance must be in place and, at the very least, third-party liability in case of a road traffic accident. You should ascertain that the insurances are in place and whether there are any excesses to pay in the case of an accident. Many schools include insurance in their prices but some do not, so don't be afraid to ask.

Bikes and equipment vary from school to school but you should expect to be supplied with equipment such as radios that work and bikes that are clean, serviced and maintained.

Because of the need to train CBT off-road you may want to enquire whether there are any refreshments available at the site and check for other essential facilities.

Most schools offer basic levels of protective equipment such as helmets, gloves and waterproofs, but again there is no harm in asking exactly what is provided for the price being charged.

Motorcycle training should be an enjoyable experience. By selecting a good training organisation you are ensuring that you receive high quality, professional training.

BSM is a trusted and well-known brand and being part of the RAC Group guarantees a high level of quality and service to all its customers. Word of mouth is another good indicator. Of course, you can read through Yellow Pages or the local newspaper but do your homework and ask the questions before you select your training school.

Most schools are competitively priced and if one is a lot cheaper than the others you must question the quality of training you may receive. Remember to ask what you are getting for your money. While dearest is not always best, cheapest can also have pitfalls. BSM prices are inclusive of all equipment and insurances and you will be told exactly what you are getting for your money, including the most important detail – how much training you will receive.

What about clothing?

No matter what size bike you are thinking of riding there is no alternative to wearing the correct clothing. While the only legal requirement in this country is an approved safety helmet, serious consideration should be given to protecting other parts of your body. At no time should you ride your bike in shorts and a t-shirt, no matter how good the weather.

Helmets
There are two basic styles of safety helmet to look out for. The most common is known as full-faced. This has a chin guard that offers protection in the case of a mishap. Full-faced helmets are also invariably fitted with an integral visor that

– Apart from the legally required safety helmet, serious consideration should be given to protecting other parts of your body.

offers eye protection in inclement weather. However, you do lose a little peripheral vision compared with the second type.

The second style of helmet is known as open-faced. This is popular in summer because it leaves the face open to the elements. But you do need to wear some form of eye protection when wearing an open-faced helmet. All helmets purchased in this country must have either a blue or green Kite mark sticker on them or conform to EU regulations.

Gloves and boots

Gloves should ideally be made from leather; specifically designed motorcycle gloves have sturdy stitching and extra protection to the palms and knuckles. Boots offer protection to the ankle and partially to the shin; again, they should be made from leather and have a sturdy sole offering good grip.

Outer garments

At the time of writing, the best abrasive resistant material on the market is still leather. Leather is durable and offers a high level of protection. However, at best it is only shower proof so a second layer of waterproof clothing is needed for all-year use.

There are alternatives to leather in the form of man-made materials that offer protection from both injury and the weather. When purchasing a protective jacket or trousers you should look for good-quality double stitching and extra layers of material on the main wear areas of the garment (knees, elbows and shoulders). Most motorcycle clothing now has built-in body armour that gives you extra security.

When buying any form of protective clothing remember to chose colours that other road users can see clearly.

How do I choose a bike?

Before you buy your new motorcycle, visit as many motorcycle show rooms as possible and look at the choice available. Talk to the staff and get some advice from people who have been riding for a while. Motorcycle and scooter magazines are a great source of information and can give you unbiased reviews of all the newest and most popular models. It is important to choose a machine that will suit your needs – there is no point in buying a small-capacity machine if you are

planning a month-long tour of the Alps! You can also talk to your instructor, who can offer sound advice on the type of machine best suited to you and your ability. Wherever possible you should ask for a test ride on the machine of your choice, after all you are making a big investment and can't be expected to part with your money before you have tried the product.

As well as motorcycle dealers you can look through one of the many publications that offer second-hand bikes for sale. Always take a friend along who knows what they are looking at when viewing prospective buys. It is very easy to be taken in by a shiny machine only to find out that it has a terminal engine problem when you get it home.

If you spend a little time researching your new pastime you will be rewarded and not buy a machine that you want to replace after a couple of weeks.